HOW TO ENJOY YOUR RETIREMENT

ACTIVITIES FROM A TO Z

Tricia Wagner • Barbara Day

VanderWyk & Burnham

ACTON, MASSACHUSETTS

Published by VanderWyk & Burnham
A Division of Publicom, Inc.
P.O. Box 2789, Acton, Massachusetts 01720

This publication is sold with the understanding that the publisher is not engaged in rendering legal, medical, or other professional services. If expert assistance is required, the services of a competent professional person should be sought.

This book is available for quantity purchases. For information on bulk discounts, call 1-800-789-7916 or write to Special Sales at the above address.

Library of Congress Cataloging-in-Publication Data
Wagner, Tricia.
    How to enjoy your retirement : activities from A to Z / Tricia Wagner, Barbara Day.
       p.   cm.
    Rev. ed. of: How to enjoy retirement. c1995.
    Includes bibliographical references and index.
    ISBN 1-889242-02-0 (pbk.)
    1. Retirement—United States—Miscellanea. 2. Aged—Recreation—United States—Miscellanea. 3. Creative activities and seat work. I. Day, Barbara. II. Wagner, Tricia. How to enjoy retirement. III. Title.
HQ1063.2.U6W34   1998
646.7'9—dc21
                                          97-48599
                                          CIP

Book design and health icon created by Dinardo Design
Pages 195–202 illustrations © Lenice Strohmeier

Manufactured in the United States of America
10 9 8 7 6 5 4 3 2 1

In memory
of Jerry Day,
beloved brother,
father,
and grandfather,
with our love
and thanks.

C O N T E N T S

FOREWORD by Steve Allen

 ive hundred years ago there would have been no need for a book such as this. Humans began dying literally the day they were born, and relatively few reached the age of 65. "Good jobs that paid fair wages" were few and far between, and there were certainly none of the medical miracles that now so greatly prolong life for millions of us.

Concerning the need for retirement itself I must largely conjecture, since I am among that fortunate minority who work in the creative arts—and those who paint, sculpt, compose, play a musical instrument, act, or write have little or no interest in retirement. Indeed, the very idea of halting the exercise of creative gifts is repugnant. It is literally absurd to suggest that a painter should put down his brushes for all time because he has reached a specific age.

The overwhelming majority of us, of course, have no such luck. We recognize that we must work if we wish to eat and be housed and clothed. There also may be others who depend on us for their support, and that provides more incentive for sticking to our job, whether we are fully pleased with it or not. But when the allegedly blessed day that we are relieved of all professional obligations finally arrives, most of us discover that it is decidedly a mixed blessing. I would think that even those who did not particularly enjoy their work, or who found it outright irksome, would not be able to go beyond the first few weeks of glorious freedom without courting boredom and uncertainty. We do not have to simply wonder about such questions; it is already clear that for some of us retirement is very far indeed from the endless round

. . . .

of golf, bridge-playing, and general vacation activity that we have read or dreamed about.

George Bernard Shaw, as apparently everyone is aware, once observed that youth is such a glorious thing that it's a shame to waste it on the young. And there's also something not quite balanced about wasting retirement on the old. Undoubtedly, we know more at 65 than we did at 25, and we may even be fortunate enough to retain that broad intellectual curiosity without which life isn't all that interesting anyway. But what all of this means is that we would be well advised to begin thinking about and planning for our retirement long before it becomes our immediate business.

Since humans vary so greatly in their tastes, I assume there can be no such thing as one simple retirement plan that will be best for all. What the authors of this wise and entertaining work have done is save the rest of us a good deal of study time. They have thought long and carefully, and consulted the views of others, about this issue of finding ourselves with "nothing to do"; we would be smart to heed their advice and to consider the options they hold out.

STEVE ALLEN
FEBRUARY 1998

AUTHORS' PREFACE

How to Enjoy Your Retirement: Activities from A to Z represents the combined efforts, ideas, and experiences not only of ourselves—Tricia Wagner and Barbara Day—but also of friends, family members, and neighbors who eagerly provided us with additional ideas for the book. Thank you to all and to those sources acknowledged on the next page, who graciously allowed us to use quotations and excerpts from their works.

Tricia got the idea for this book when a friend lamented, "What am I going to do when I retire?" A search of Denver's library and bookstores turned up no direct answers to that question. Here was a perfect "find a need and fill it" situation. About this time, Tricia's nephew and his wife, Barbara, arrived in Denver. We began collaborating on a list of activities for retired people, which took on a life of its own as it grew into this book.

How to Enjoy Your Retirement is written for both men and women. We avoid using the term *spouse* and instead use the terms *partner* and *significant other* because of the varied living arrangements in society today and our desire to include everyone. Those of you on computers will be glad to see we have often included website and e-mail addresses for companies and organizations named in our text.

We do need to ask for your understanding when you find out that a phone number has been disconnected or has a new area code, a company's mail-forwarding order has expired, a website no longer exists, a book has gone out of print or now costs more money—and so on. The world will keep changing in between editions of this book, but

· ·

we'll try to keep up! You can help by letting us know any time you learn of a fact in this book that is no longer true. Write to us c/o VanderWyk & Burnham, P.O. Box 2789, Acton, MA 01720.

We thoroughly enjoyed putting this book together. By no means do we pretend to have covered everything. We offer a sprinkling of what's out there. We hope these ideas will contribute to happy and fulfilling retirement "careers" for our readers.

Finally, in acknowledgment, we would like to thank Meredith Rutter, our publisher at VanderWyk & Burnham, and Cynthia Nye, our editor, for their enthusiasm, expertise, and guidance in bringing this project to completion and making it a reality. Also, for the kind permission to use material from the following sources, we thank Paul and Gail Dennison for *Brain Gym®*, Edu-Kinesthetics, Inc., P.O. Box 3396, Ventura, CA 93006; *Denver Post*, 1560 Broadway, Denver, CO 80202; *Handbook of Inspirational and Motivational Stories, Anecdotes and Humor*, by Winston K. Pendleton; *Maturity News Service*, National Press Building, Suite 968, Washington, DC 20045; *Orange County Register*, 625 N. Grand Avenue, Santa Ana, CA 92701; *21st Century Dictionary of Quotations*, edited by The Princeton Language Institute, produced by The Philip Lief Group, Inc. (Bantam Doubleday/Dell Publishing Group).

TRICIA WAGNER AND BARBARA DAY
JANUARY 1998

I N T R O D U C T I O N

You have worked somewhere between ten and fifty years, and RETIRE-MENT looms ahead. People face retirement with a variety of feelings, including excitement, anxiety, fear, and trepidation. If you have hobbies, you may be able to slip into retirement without missing a beat. If you do not have an all-consuming hobby, you may need some new interests and activities to enrich your retirement hours.

That's where this book comes into your life. These pages contain hundreds of ideas and activities, presented in alphabetical order, to jostle your mind into renewed creativity. Before you get to the *A* to *Z* of it, read the advice on taking a personal inventory of your retirement needs and desires (see section on next page). Also think about the importance of getting along with a significant other if you will now be together a lot more. Read the communication tips on pages 7–12.

The book's larger *A* to *Z* section — "Get in the Swing with These" — describes hundreds of ideas in varying degrees of detail (pages 13–111). If you're determined to stay physically healthy, look for the health icon that appears next to appropriate ideas in this section. Once warmed up by the "Swing" ideas, you can "Let Your Imagination Soar" with the next *A* to *Z* section: a smorgasbord of bare-bones topics to stimulate additional activity ideas (pages 113–181).

The first appendix (pages 183–188) provides the questions for taking a personal inventory. Remaining appendices explore the possibilities of spending time with your grandchildren (pages 189–193), doing exercises to synchronize your body and your brain (pages 195–203), starting a small business (pages 205–208), volunteering in your community or around the world (pages 209–214), and traveling afar (pages 215–240). Additional information resources (pages 241–250) and reading suggestions (pages 251–253) are also included.

We hope, by the power of suggestion, to enable you to plumb the depths of your mind and soul, to awaken the real you, to energize the creative mind that perhaps has lain dormant until this time in your life. Use this book as your private retirement planner. Only you can answer the questions and make the choices. If this is your own copy, there is plenty of space to jot down comments and note any sparks of interest. *How to Enjoy Your Retirement: Activities from A to Z* is as close to a magic formula as you can find. You may be surprised how many of these ideas blossom into meaningful and rewarding activities. It's all up to you!

Taking a Personal Inventory

Why do a personal inventory? Why not? Retirement is an ending and a beginning. The personal inventory can be your preface to an exciting new life. If you honestly answer the questions in Appendix A, you will have a better understanding of your past and present support system, interests, and relationships; where you want to live; why you are retiring; how you are going to pay for retirement; and whether there are things or people needing repair or attention in your life.

In Appendix A, "Who Are You?" (pages 183–184) helps you to explore your ancestry, family relationships, religion, leisure activities, and social connections. "What Have You Done? What Do You Do Well?" (page 184) explores talents and past successes. "When Will or Did You Retire?" (page 185) asks about your retirement schedule and your relationship with any significant other from the angle of perhaps being together a lot more now. "Where Will You Live?" (pages 185–186) raises the possibility of a move and travel plans. "Why Are You Retiring?" (page 186) explores your reason(s) for retirement and any special considerations you may have. "How Will You Pay for Retirement?" (pages 186–187) assesses income sources and options. "Determining Your Net Worth" (pages 187–188) reviews your assets and debts to identify exactly what you have to work with financially.

Overall, your inventory may introduce you to another you, one who has been repressed or overlooked for years. Wake up the real you! You are on the brink of a new adventure called *retirement*. Dip your toes in the water. Take notes from pages 115–181 and turn them into your "wish list." Be inventive, playful, even frivolous. What do you really want? What do you want the rest/best of your life to be?

THE COMMODORE'S PRAYER

Lord, thou knowest better than I know myself that I am growing older and will someday be old. Keep me from the fatal habit of thinking I must say something on every subject and on every occasion. Release me from craving to straighten out everybody's affairs. Make me thoughtful but not moody, helpful but not bossy. With my vast store of wisdom, it seems a pity not to use it all, but Thou knowest, Lord, that I want a few friends at the end.

Keep my mind free from the recital of endless details; give me wings to get to the point. Seal my lips on my aches and pains. They are increasing, and love of rehearsing them is becoming sweeter as the years go by. I dare not ask for grace enough to enjoy the tales of others' pains, but help me to endure them with patience.

I dare not ask for improved memory but for a growing humility and a lessening cocksureness when my memory seems to clash with the memories of others. Teach me the glorious lesson that occasionally I may be mistaken.

Keep me reasonably sweet; I do not want to be a Saint—some of them are so hard to live with—but a sour old person is one of the crowning works of the devil. Give me the ability to see good things in unexpected places and talents in unexpected people. And give me, Lord, the grace to tell them so. Amen.

Author Unknown

GETTING ALONG WITH EACH OTHER: COMMUNICATION TIPS

Many years ago, a friend and co-worker gave Tricia some advice on how to communicate with colleagues. We have found the advice so effective, both at work and in personal relationships, that we want to share it with you in this section of communication tips.

Suppose somebody has made a mistake on something they have written. You know they've done it wrong, but you also know people are likely to be offended when told bluntly, "You've made a mistake here. This is wrong!" A more tactful comment might be, "Am I reading this right?" or "Would you explain this to me?" or "This doesn't seem quite right to me. Is there something I'm missing?" This approach gives the other person a chance to correct the mistake without feeling personally attacked.

To see the possibilities of tactful communication in a personal relationship, think about driving—often a source of conflict for couples. Imagine that you and your partner are in a car, and your partner is driving. Neither of you has ever been where you're heading, and you know that your partner is likely to get lost but hates to be told how to drive. So you might raise the question early: "What's the best way to get there?" Together you can discuss the best route for the time of day or conditions. Then about five blocks before it's time to turn and your car is in the wrong lane, ask, "Are we supposed to turn soon?" or "Is that our turn coming up?" This averts the possibly ugly consequences of driving by the turn. What you are doing is nudging without nagging or accusing.

O PROMISE ME

O promise me

That when the first intense excitement has died away, and the first bright luster of our association has dulled, you will recall that this was your idea as much as mine.

That you will always believe me to be the most desirable, and that the appearance of possession will not lull that desire into sleep.

That our dreams of a 'different' marriage can still come true, if we both but try, and keep on trying.

You will remember the time you said, "It takes two to quarrel," and I answered you, "Yes, and it takes two to get along."

You will once more meditate on the theories we expounded in soft, hushed tones—that marriage merely gave us an option on each other, and both of us would try to keep that option desirable above all things.

You will forever believe that those 'magic words' were truly magic, and while they granted no rights, they blessed and sanctioned our privileges.

You will never forget that I am just a human being, possessed of all the frailties and faults which love once glossed over.

You will never fail to grant me the kindnesses you extend so willingly to your most casual friends.

And that, as the years roll by, you will often say, I love you more—and more—and more.

As I have promised you.

Author Unknown

Know the difference between backseat driving and selective strategic navigating. Depending on the preference of the driver making a turn, it may be okay for the passenger to say, "You're fine on my side" or "You're clear after this red minivan." Sometimes it takes two to drive safely. Talk it over. If the driver doesn't want help, keep quiet unless there is danger of an accident.

Is one member of your household tidy and one member messy? Retirement can bring on arguments about how tidy the house needs to be. Just remember that neither of you is likely to change completely. If each gives a little, maybe you can reach a happy medium. Also, identify the chores you each like to do, and share all the other jobs around the house.

If both you and your significant other are retired, you may be spending much more time together than you did before retirement. Hopefully, clear, considerate communication has been an important part of your relationship all along. If not, problems may develop as the days go by. Sometimes one partner ends up spending time away from home just to stay out of the other person's way. Make it a priority to work out differences and reach resolutions before small conflicts grow into larger barriers between you. Discuss how much time you want to spend together and how much time you each want to spend alone or with other friends. It can be miserable trying to occupy the same house all day every day without making some determination about togetherness. We firmly believe that as long as the two of you work together, you can work wonders. When you work against each other, everything falls apart.

L*et there be spaces in your togetherness.*

—Kahlil Gibran

If your partner is still working outside the home, he or she may have special needs, such as more spending money or fewer household responsibilities. On the other hand, if your partner is also retired or has

GOLDEN RULES FOR EASIER LIVING

1. If you open it, close it.

2. If you turn it on, turn it off.

3. If you unlock it, lock it up.

4. If you break it, admit it.

5. If you can't fix it, call in someone who can.

6. If you borrow it, return it.

7. If you value it, take care of it.

8. If you make a mess, clean it up.

9. If you move it, put it back.

10. If it belongs to someone else and you want to use it, get permission.

11. If you don't know how to operate it, leave it alone.

12. If it's none of your business, don't ask questions.

13. If it ain't broke, don't fix it.

14. If it will brighten someone's day—SAY IT!

Author Unknown

been home all along, you both will have adjustments to make now that you are home full-time, too.

Regarding busy work, it's amazing how things to do will expand to fill up the time available. Make sure you really need or want to do all these things and are not just finding busy work.

Also, avoid speaking for your partner. For example, don't say, "I'm sure Bill will be happy to work on your car" (or whatever) when Bill may have a dozen other things he would rather be doing. Check with the other person first. You might say, "He keeps pretty busy now that he's retired" or "She keeps her own schedule. I'll ask her." Don't volunteer your significant other's time or services without first consulting them.

Both parties need to know how to shop for groceries, do the wash, operate the microwave, write checks, balance the checkbook, and manage investments. Both parties need to know about the cars, maintenance schedules, location of keys and titles, all insurance policies, each other's valuable collections, lawn equipment, jewelry, discharge papers, wills and living wills (which you should carry with you when you travel), final wishes, and funeral plans.

When speaking to each other, particularly in the presence of others, try to avoid using harsh voice inflections. Discuss your dissatisfactions in private and try to come to understandings that will work for both of you. Keep in mind the maxim, "It's not what you say, it's how you say it."

If you need help developing communication skills in your relationship, don't be afraid to seek assistance, whether it be through joining a program at your place of worship, reading books or listening to tapes on communication and relationships, or going to a professional counselor. Good communication between you and your significant other will definitely enhance your retirement.

Once a woman has forgiven her man, she must not reheat his sins for breakfast.

—Marlene Dietrich

Finally, have consideration for the memory lapses, foibles, idiosyncrasies, and infirmities we all have that may become more pronounced as we grow older.

A true conception of the relation of the sexes will not admit of conqueror and conquered; it knows of but one great thing; to give one's self boundlessly in order to find oneself richer, deeper and better.

—Emma Goldman

GET IN THE SWING WITH THESE

ACTIVITIES FROM

A TO Z

Adopt a Highway — Colorado has a wonderful volunteer program through which groups of people clean litter from the highways. Contact your state highway department to see if they have such a program. If not, inquire about starting one. If you would like information on Colorado's Adopt-a-Highway Program, for instance, call 1-303-757-9514 or 1-303-757-9536.

Adopt a Native-American Grandparent — Lakota Indian elders are often raising their grandchildren because of alcoholism and high unemployment on the reservations. The grandparents can be "adopted" by volunteers and helped financially with such things as propane, warm clothing, groceries, and electricity bills. You can send anything your adopted family needs right to their home. One grandpa likes to garden, so his sponsor sends him seeds. One grandma's grandchildren are about the same age as her sponsor's children, so that sponsor sends "hand-me-down" clothing as her own children outgrow still-good clothes. Some of the grandparents sell quilts or other crafts made with donated materials. Donors enjoy the one-to-one contact with the elders. Contact the Adopt-a-Grandparent Program, P.O. Box 241, Taos, NM 87571.

Adoption Open Records — Find your long-lost relatives. Try the World Wide Registry (http://www.phoenix.net/~aquarian/davids/birth.html) and Find Me Reunion Registry (http://www.findme-registry.com). Good luck and have fun!

Aging Family Members — If you have someone in your home who needs care, several helpful sources offer information on this subject. Obtain the *Complete Elder Care Planner* by Joy Loverde (Hyperion, $14.95) or *Helping Yourself Help Others* by Rosalynn Carter (Times Books/Random House, $14.00). Rosalynn Carter's book talks about giving care, handling isolation, and avoiding burnout. It also refers to helpful organizations. The United Seniors Health Cooperative has published *Home Care for Older People*. Their address is 1331 H Street, NW, Suite 500, Washington, DC 20005. The book costs approximately $12. Also, on the Web, take a look at http://www.caregiver.com .

Airplanes — The next time you make a flight reservation, think about the direction you'll be traveling. Try to reserve a seat on the shady side of the plane to avoid the sun's glare.

Alcohol and Drugs — For a fact sheet on alcohol and drugs and associated domestic violence, call the National Clearing House for Alcohol and Drug Information, 1-800-729-6686 (or http://www.health.org/index.html).

Alzheimer's Disease — Get free fact sheets on Alzheimer's disease, a Caregiver Resource List, and local support group information by contacting the Alzheimer's Disease Education and Referral Center (ADEAR) at 1-800-438-4380 (or http://www.cais.com/adear/index.html). For additional information, contact The Alzheimer Association at 1-800-272-3900 or The French Foundation for Alzheimer's Research at 1-800-477-2243.

American Association of Retired Persons — Join the AARP and enjoy the many benefits they offer. Annual membership dues are $8 for one year, $20 for three years, and $45 for ten years. This includes 85¢ for an annual subscription to the *AARP Bulletin* and $2.40 for *Modern Maturity* magazine. Send to AARP Membership Center, P.O. Box 199, Long Beach, CA 80901. For AARP's group health insurance plans, call 1-800-245-1212. For AARP pharmacy services, call 1-800-439-4461. For AARP's investment program through Scudder Funds, call 1-800-322-2282. AARP is now online (http://www.aarp.org/). Computer users can receive news and information about the association and share opinions and views.

Animation/Computer Skills — Draw digital animated characters with a computer. You may discover a marketable skill, and Hollywood may want you! Places to look for jobs include Sony Pictures Imageworks, Dreamworks Animation, Klasky Csupo, HBO Animation, Walt Disney Television Animation, Pacific Data Images, Nickelodeon's Nicktoons, Industrial Light & Magic, and Fox Animation Studios. For company addresses, check the information desk at your local library for *American Business Location Directory* or *American Business Disk* or the *Million Dollar Directory*. Also, you could check ads in current animation magazines (bookstores, library, newsstands).

Aquariums — What could be more fun or relaxing than a beautiful aquarium? For complete aquarium systems including the stand, lights, and filters (all you add is fish), contact Surgarium, Inc., 6732 West Coal Mine Avenue, Unit 20, Littleton, CO 80123, or call 1-303-324-5255. The fax number is 1-303-738-0252. These units use a new filter design called algae scrubbers and have a surging device that makes waves in the aquarium. For aquarium parts and filtration systems, contact MMFI Aquaricare Division, P.O. Box 37531, Denver, CO 80237, or call 1-303-478-7093. The fax number is 1-303-979-9069. They manufacture a broad range of products, primarily filtration systems including algae scrubbers.

Archaeological Dig—At thousands of sites throughout the U.S., archaeologists uncover delicate and ancient artifacts from America's past. Volunteers of all ages are often welcome to help. To find a dig near you, contact your state historical society or request the Archaeological Fieldwork Opportunities Bulletin, a publication of the Archaeological Institute of America, Department AFOB, 675 Commonwealth Avenue, Boston, MA 02215 (1-617-353-9361).

Archery—Consider taking up archery as a hobby.

A*rt is the only way to run away without leaving home.*

—Twyla Tharp

Art—Have you always had a love of art? Visit art museums and art exhibits. Start collecting art. Study art history.

Art Car Weekend—Attend an Art Car Weekend, held in Houston in April. People paint their cars to represent everything from fruits and vegetables to dreamy, celestial, glow-in-the-dark murals. Often, the artists dress to match their cars. One man has a long-horned steer for a hood ornament. He says, "When I pass a pasture, even the cows look up." For more information, contact Houston's Chamber of Commerce (1-713-923-7989).

Art Gallery on Wheels—Create an art gallery on wheels. One man we've read about has turned his minivan into an art gallery he calls "Gallery Van Go." He tore out the seats, paneling, and carpet to make room for the artwork and had a second battery installed to power lights for the art exhibits. He has several artists lined up for "Van Go" exhibits in coming months.

Artifacts—Study the artifacts of North America. Some that have been discovered in several sites near the Wisconsin-Illinois line may be as old as or predate Mayan artifacts found in Monte Verde, Chile. Other old sites include Clovis, New Mexico; Meadowcroft, near Pittsburgh—the site of a rock shelter some believe was used by hunters 19,000 years ago; and the Yukon Territory's Old Crow site, where archaeologists  dug up bone tools that could be 27,000 years old. Contact the archaeology department in a local college or state university or inquire at the library.

Artists—Do you work with watercolor, oils, acrylics, or mixed media? Enter your artwork in a juried art competition, such as the one held each fall in Cheyenne, Wyoming. For a prospectus, send a #10 self-addressed, stamped envelope to Cheyenne Artists Guild File X, 1010 East Sixteenth Street, Cheyenne, WY 82001. Also, an organization called Arts Are Alive Over 55 stages senior art shows around the country. If there is not a show in your area, why not start one?

Arts and Crafts Worldwide—Buy handmade, one-of-a-kind items, made by craftspeople in more than thirty Third World countries, at a 10,000 Villages Shop. They have banana-fiber animals from Kenya; colorful, handwoven table linens from India; Indonesian shadow puppets; and oversized blue-and-white Vietnamese flowerpots. This shop, found in different cities, is a nonprofit store staffed by volunteers. If you like to shop by mail, order a catalog of catalogs from Publisher Inquiry Services at P.O. Box 3099, Boca Raton, FL 33431 or call 1-407-998-9722. One catalog that offers global clothing and gifts is The Planet; call 1-800-324-5950 and ask for a free catalog.

Astronomers — Become a backyard astronomer under the direction of Columbia University astronomer Joe Patterson. His program, called the Center for Backyard Astrophysics, includes amateurs in eleven countries on six continents. The backyard astronomers record data and send it to Joe Patterson via computer. More than 300,000 amateur astronomers worldwide belong to similar clubs. Some clubs have gone as far as to pool money to buy highly sophisticated equipment. For example, Thomas Droege of Batavia, Illinois, has spent $50,000 to build telescope cameras that he gives away to amateurs who join his group of backyard observers. Contact Joe Patterson at Columbia University, 212 Hamilton Hall, New York, NY 10027 (1-212-854-2522).

Authors — Do you know any authors? Have area writers been featured in your local newspaper? Ask them to give a talk about their works. Charge a small admission to cover refreshments.

Autobiography — Would you like to write an autobiography? *The Book of Myself* by Carl and David Marshall (Hyperion, $14.95) is a do-it-yourself book of 201 questions that prompt you to record your personal habits and traits, your history, your wisdom, and the stories you want to share with future generations. Answer the question on each page, and your story is told!

Automobiles — If you want to get rid of a used vehicle, consider donating it to the Boys and Girls Clubs, which fix up and sell the cars to raise money to fund their programs. Check your local telephone directory for a chapter in your state. If automobiles interest you (as they do Tricia's husband, Bill, who provided this section), there are many ways to enjoy this hobby. You can get into detailing, which would require some training. Go to a detail shop and learn how they do it. Many shops are willing to share their trade secrets. You can buy, sell, or trade cars as a dealer or wholesaler. This may require working with a dealership as a salesperson for a period of time, or working with another wholesaler. You can collect cars or join a car club (see below).

Collect Cars: Buy and sell collector vehicles. Trading collector cars successfully requires some schooling and research to learn the market. Several useful publications, such as *Hemmings Motor News, Old Cars Weekly,* and others, are available at newsstands. Getting started also might require an outlay of between $3,000 and $100,000. To learn more about collector cars, become acquainted with a person in the old-car hobby who is willing to teach you. Attend some old-car auctions, just to watch and listen. It takes time to become familiar with the market. The address for *Hemmings Motor News* is P.O. Box 1108, Bennington, VT 05201 (1-800-227-4373, ext. 550). *Old Cars Weekly News & Marketplace* is published by Krause Publications, Inc., 700 East State Street, Iola, WI 54990; call 1-715-445-2214 or fax at 1-715-445-4087. Kruse (not Krause) Auctions hold collector-car auctions all over the country throughout the year. For a free color brochure of the Kruse Auctions, or to sell a collector car, write to P.O. Box 190, 5540 C.R. 11-A, Auburn, IN 46706, or call 1-800-968-4444. Kruse is also online (http://www.kruseinternational.com) or use their e-mail address (info@kruseinternational.com).

Car Clubs: Join a car club if you own just about any car made before 1970. You can pick from the Horseless Carriage Club, the Falcon Club, or the Thunderbird Club. There are the Studebaker, Early V-8, Model-T, and Corvette Clubs, and hundreds of others.  Members have fun with car-related activities and social events. Contact a dealership that sells your kind of car. They probably know of a related car club. Activities are sometimes listed in local newspapers, or try the telephone book Yellow Pages under *Clubs.* If you're going to store an old car for any length of time, add gas stabilizer to the gas tank and put moth balls and D-Con around to keep mice from eating your wiring and upholstery.

Automobile Insurance — Get the government publication titled *Consumer's Independent Guide to Auto Insurance,* a 44-page guide (free!) that makes it easy to understand your insurance needs and the options available. Call 1-800-261-4422.

Automobile Lease — Lease a car, but insist on a closed-end lease instead of an open-end lease. In a closed-end lease, you are not locked in to buying the car at the end of the lease, and you are not responsible for coming up with the difference when the car is worth less than you owe at the end of the lease.

Babyography — Order a "Babyography," a distinctive keepsake for your grandchild's room. It contains a dozen facts about the baby's birth, including date, time, weight, length, hair color, doctor's name, and parents' names, as well as the child's astrological sign, names of other famous people who share the child's birthday, and a time capsule of current headlines. The 11 x 14-inch certificate costs $16.95 plus shipping. A framed "Babyography" costs $44.95. Call 1-800-781-7171.

Back Trouble — If you have trouble with your back, order a catalog from the BackSaver Products Company, 53 Jeffrey

Avenue, Holliston, MA 01746, or call 1-800-251-2225. On the East Coast visit JoAnne's Bed and Back shops and the Healthy Back Store. Relax the Back is in Texas, and the Better Back Store is in ten western states.

Baldness—Shop for baldness remedies. Choices include Propecia, Rogaine, or Kevas at 1-800-245-HAIR (245-4247). Dr. Christiane Northrup had an extensive article on how to remedy hair loss in her May 1997 issue of *Health Wisdom for Women* newsletter. Subscriptions to the newsletter are available through Phillips Publishing, Inc. (1-800-211-8561) at a cost of $69 per year—well worth the price since it is full of helpful information, especially for women.

Bed and Breakfast—For bed-and-breakfast information, you may call one toll-free phone number (1-800-US-BandB or 872-2632), between 8:00 A.M. and 5:00 P.M. Pacific time. A computer printout listing lodgings priced from $35 to $350 a night and located near a specified destination will be mailed or faxed to you. If you enjoy meeting people and don't mind putting yourself into your work, consider owning and operating your own bed-and-breakfast inn, which can be a very interesting business.

Beer—Open a brew pub of your own, or just create your own family recipe.

Bird Hunting/Watching—Get a good dog and a few friends and go on a bird hunting trip. If you're interested in bird watching, join the National Audubon Society. Read the book *All the Birds of North America*, a new field guide beautifully designed and written by Jack L. Riggs for the American Bird Conservancy (Harper, $19.95). In this book, illustrations are grouped under color-coded icons representing the birds' feeding behavior and easily recognizable features. You may want to install bird feeders in your yard. Stock the feeders with black-oil type sunflower, white proso millet, niger or thistle seed, suet, or fruit. Become a member of the National Bird Feeding Society, Box 23, Northbrook, IL 60065. Membership is $15 per year and includes six issues of the *Bird's Eye reView* newsletter.

Birth Order—Study the interesting hypotheses presented in *Born to Rebel: Birth Order, Family Dynamics and Creative Lives* by Frank J. Sulloway (Random House, $30.00). He describes the different traits and behavior patterns characteristic of first-born, middle-born, and later-born children. Do you and people you know fit his profiles?

Book Club—Start or join a book club to read and discuss books every month. Eating and socializing can be part of this wonderful pastime.

Book Storage—Follow the lead of the Library of Congress and increase your book storage space by one-third: Sort books by their sizes so shelves can be raised or lowered. The Library of Congress also gives away thousands of duplicate or unneeded books to nonprofit groups. You have to travel to the Washington, DC, library to select the books. Write to the Library of Congress, Exchange and Gift Division, Madison Building, 101 Independence Avenue, SE, Room B-03, Washington, DC 20540.

E*verybody wants to do something to help, but nobody wants to be first.*

—Pearl Bailey

Books and Tapes for the Blind—The National Library Service for the Blind and Physically Handicapped produces recorded and Braille books and magazines. Of the thirty million Americans over sixty-five, many are temporarily or permanently unable to read print. They now have access to more than 676,000 biographies, bestsellers, classics, mysteries, romance novels, and poetry books. Joe Volz, with the *Maturity News Service,* writes: "The talking books and magazines are narrated by professionals and produced on cassette tapes or flexible disc records. Local libraries lend out the books, along with easy-to-use equipment. Readers can participate directly from home by postage-free mail. Books and equipment are all loaned free, and easy-to-operate machines are also loaned free." For more information, contact your local library or senior center.

Books on Tape — Listen to books while driving or jogging. The audiobook market has grown 70 percent since 1990; as we write this book, more than 50,000 titles are available. For a sampling, call 1-888-AUDIO-99 (1-888-283-4699). The website is http://www.areyoulistening.com . Another phone number is 1-800-88BOOKS (882-6657). Many bookstores carry audiobooks.

Boredom — Fight boredom by trying something new. Maybe you'll like it!

Braille Printing — Donate or raise money to buy computers to help speed braille printing done in Boston, Massachusetts; Chicago, Illinois; Louisville, Kentucky; Stewart, Florida; and the Jenny Beck Braille Center in Philadelphia, Pennsylvania. The Beck Center uses these computers, which have revolutionized the printing process. At the other locations, printing is slow and laborious, done on just a six-key typewriter called a Braillewriter. Also, do you have any ideas to make paper money easier to use for the blind person? To share your ideas, contact the Bureau of Printing and Engraving at 1-202-874-2361.

Brainstorm — Do this with others to find something to do. That's the way this book got started. One little comment — "What will I do when I retire?" — took fire and turned into this book.

Bridge — Play bridge. It's a wonderful way to meet people and stimulate your brain.

Few men during their lifetime come anywhere near exhausting the resources dwelling within them. There are deep wells of strength that are never used.

—Admiral Richard E. Byrd

Bug Zapper — Throw away your bug zapper. It kills more good bugs than it kills biting bugs, according to a study by the University of Delaware at Newark, New Jersey.

"Build a Generation" — Colorado has a crime prevention concept to identify risks in a community. When these risks can be reduced or eliminated in the community, the incidence of delinquency and criminal behavior is reduced. For more information, call 1-303-239-4471.

Bumper Stickers — Enjoy deciphering license plates and reading bumper stickers. Paul Rosa decided the latter were too safe and too boring. He dreamed up some satire on wheels with his first sticker, "My Kid Beat Up Your Honor Student." Rosa's bumper sticker sells at the rate of 40,000 per year. Now he is peddling his satire through Spencer Gifts, with 500 outlets around the country. Rosa's website is http://www.idiot-ink.com .

Bungee Jumping — It's free in some places for those over seventy years of age.

Butter Substitute—Kristine Bateman developed a low-fat substitute for butter with only 13 grams of fat per cup instead of the 176 grams of fat in real butter. Order this butter substitute by calling 1-800-574-6822.

Camp for Blind Kids—Investigate a Camp for Blind Kids. Call 1-888-554-KIDS (1-888-554-5437). How can you become involved?

Camping—Take either short trips or extended camping excursions. Enjoy the campgrounds when they're not crowded with holiday and weekend campers.

Cancer—Change your diet and you can potentially escape some cancers. Everything we read suggests it is a good idea to eat less fat and increase your intake of fruits and vegetables. Stop smoking, keep your weight down, and limit your alcohol intake to only one or two small drinks a day. If you are a licensed cosmetologist or hairdresser, you can give makeup suggestions, skin and nail care tips, and ideas on how to wear wigs and scarves to women undergoing chemotherapy or radiation and coping with hair loss. This program was founded by the Cosmetic, Toiletry, and Fragrance Association, supported by the National Cosmetology Association and the American Cancer Society. Call 1-800-227-2345.

Candles — Use candles for something besides lighting or romance. Now people are using candles for everything from home decor and aroma therapy to meditation and spiritual practice. Candles are to the '90s what crystals were to the '80s. A new retail and mail order store called Illuminations has everything from white votive candles ($6.00 per dozen) to large, colored aroma therapy pillars ($75.00). They have stores in Santa Clara and Corte Madera, California; Chicago, Illinois; Denver, Colorado; and they opened ten new stores nationwide in 1997. Coventry Creations, a company-based shop in Clinton Township, Michigan, makes a line of candles that contain herbs, oils, and blessings. Some say that lighting a candle is a way of letting go, of giving yourself permission to get rid of negativity.

Cane — If you need to use a cane, how about a clear plastic cane you can insert something decorative into? Entrepreneur Florence Foster, now in her nineties, sells clear canes that customers can fill with anything from tiny silk roses to fishing flies. Contact her at 1-888-768-9280 or 1-888-547-6240. The price is $59.50, which includes shipping.

Carp — Join the Carp Anglers Group headed by Bud Yancey, 425 Northern Oaks Drive, Groveland, IL 61535 (1-309-387-2277). Along the Mississippi River, fish markets sell smoked carp, carp jerky, and even carp bologna. "It is healthy for you," says Mike Schafer of Schafer's Fish Market in Fulton, Illinois. "We're working on a hot dog and polish sausage made of carp." Carp are also great sport fish.

Casket — Buy your casket while you're still living, from Direct Casket of Van Nuys, California. They sell caskets at a 30–70 percent discount.

The cheapest model is the Congressional, a felt-covered, corrugated cardboard casket priced at $245. Or splurge on a mahogany model for just under $1,000. Direct Casket has opened new show rooms in New York and Costa Mesa, California. Similar companies exist in other states.

Castles/Churches — Buy a vacant castle or church in Amsterdam, Netherlands, Britain, France, Germany, or elsewhere in northern Europe. Convert it into a library, a shop, a cultural center, an apartment, or a discotheque.

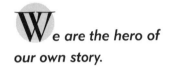

We are the hero of our own story.

—Marlene Dietrich

Cellular Phones — Check out the cellular phone world. All kinds of phones and plans can be found in electronic stores, through your local phone company, and even in the supermarket. The plans vary as to monthly rates, time-of-day restrictions, and price per minute. The phones themselves range in size from fairly lightweight to almost weightless. In an emergency, your cell phone can be priceless.

Ceramics/Paint Bar — Buy clean, white, bisque ceramic houseware items in a paint bar. Paint them into masterpieces of your own, and the paint bar will fire and glaze the items for you. Schedule a special time at a paint bar with your friends to make a whole dinner set, or whatever you want to make.

Chatty Cathy — Get your Chatty Cathy doll fixed. Kelly McIntyre of Los Angeles started repairing Chatty Cathy dolls when he was looking for ways to fight boredom at home following a bout with diabetes. He bought a supply of parts from a woman named Kathy Lewis, who had saved them from Mattel's trash barrels. Chatty Cathy's website is http://www.ttinet.com/chattycathy. Chatty Cathy even has a fan club (P.O. Box 140, Readington, NJ 08870).

Checklist for Leaving the House—Make a verbal or written checklist for leaving the house. If you're getting more absent-minded (and most of us do as we age), you'll be glad you have a checklist. Before leaving the house, have you turned everything off—the iron, the lights, the stove? Have you turned everything on—the alarm system, the lights, a radio—whatever you use for security? Do you have everything you need—money, keys (house and car), gas in the car, whatever you're taking with you (present, prizes, potluck dish, clothing, tickets), directions and a phone number for where you're going? Did you plan your round trip logically to save gas and time? Do you need to stop somewhere on the way? Do you need to pick somebody up? What about on the way back?

Childcare—Helping out in a childcare center for a business near you might be interesting part-time work. Ask what licensing or training you may need.

Children—Take your favorite little ones to a petting zoo. Fix them up with Halloween costumes and go out trick-or-treating. Encourage any talents the children demonstrate. You will be drawn together when you attend their baptisms, their First Communions, and their graduations. Go to their ball games and cheer for them, ache for them in their hurts, and celebrate with them their victories. Being with children can show us how to play again, how to laugh and hug. Take a look also at Appendix B, Spending Time with Grandchildren.

 Chinese Medicine—Learn about traditional Chinese therapies, including acupuncture. Some insurance companies cover acupuncture. For information, visit the website at http://www.acupuncture.com/ .

Chocolate—Enjoy a chocolate bar! For your information, dark chocolate contains the least amount of fat.

Chuppie—Find a way to sell something to a chuppie. *Chuppie* is a nickname for the latest new type of consumer, the mainland Chinese yuppie. In China, new magazines called "Trends Gentleman" and "Trends Lady" tell readers about the beautiful life they can enjoy by spending their new wealth on cars, expensive liqueurs, and European designer clothes. Perhaps you can capitalize on this market.

City and County Governments—Volunteer in the planning and zoning department of your city or county government, or work as a school crossing guard.

W*ho knows? Somewhere out in this audience may even be someone who will one day follow in my footsteps and preside over the White House as the President's spouse. I wish him well!*

—Barbara Bush

Clean House Naturally—Make homemade products for doing easy, cheap, and toxic-free cleaning. Get *Clean House, Clean Planet* by Karen Logan (Simon & Schuster, $12.00). She gives recipes using basic ingredients like club soda, olive oil, vinegar, and baking soda, which do not contribute to indoor air pollution. She advises against concocting your own recipes because mixing two safe ingredients may give unsafe results. You can also contact a Shaklee or similar distributor for environmentally safe cleaning products.

Closets—Clean out your closets. Consider having them professionally organized by a company specializing in closets. How would you find one? Buy the book *Clutter's Last Stand* by Don Aslett (F&W Publishers, $11.99).

Clothing— Sort through your clothing. Once retired, you won't need many power suits. Consider selling them at a near-new shop. They must be clean and in style. Start whittling down your wardrobe before retirement if possible. Think of all the money you'll save on dry cleaning. Shop for your new, casual washable clothes at discount stores, thrift shops, and garage sales. Did you throw your shirts away when you lost a button? No more. Keep your clothes in good repair. Sew on buttons and mend rips before they become huge. If you are a dancer or like parties, you'll want some nice clothes. If you need a suit for a special occasion, rent one from the same place you rent formal wear.

> **I** *did not have three thousand pairs of shoes; I had one thousand and sixty.*
>
> **—Imelda Marcos**

Clowning— Learn to be a clown. It can be lots of fun. Join the Shriners' clown group or be independent. Entertain at children's parties. Can you do magic tricks? Can you twist balloons into doggies? Do you enjoy children? If you love making people laugh and enjoy traveling, try out for the Ringling Brothers and Barnum and Bailey Clown College. Call 1-800-755-9637.

Clubs— Join Kiwanis, Rotary International, the Republicans or the Democrats, a car club, a book club, et cetera.

Coaching— Coach children's sports teams. Local schools and city parks and recreation departments are always looking for volunteers to coach different sporting events for kids.

Coffee—This is big right now, especially fancy coffees. Is it too late to open a coffee shop or coffee house? Would it be feasible? Would it be profitable? Would it be fun?

Collecting—People collect all sorts of things, from souvenir spoons to roosters to antiques to collector cars, and the list is endless! There are books available for most hobbies to help you with your collection. Following is just a taste of the collecting world.

Antique Collecting: Antiques can be fun to collect, refurbish, use, buy, sell, auction, and look for everywhere. Collecting antiques can also be profitable. For more information about antiques, check your local library for books on this subject. Also watch the newspaper for scheduled antique shows. Are you a "jukebox junkie" or "pinball wizard"?

Doll Houses and Miniatures: Visit the Doll House and Toy Museum, founded by Flora Gill Jacobs in Washington, DC.

Toys: Collecting toys is a popular and growing hobby for people of all ages. There are several categories. Cars, trucks, planes, and trains seem to go together, with different types to pick from, such as plastic, die cast, tin plate, and cast iron. Collecting toys is a fairly inexpensive hobby. Ask at your local hobby shop about clubs for toy collectors. They will probably have several publications, also. Most people collect the toys they loved and played with as children.

Collection Service—Start a debt collection service for doctors' offices, law firms, or other businesses.

Composing—Compose poetry, lyrics for music, a short story, or a novel. Try submitting your work to a local publication.

A beautiful line of verse has twelve feet, and two wings.

—Jules Renard

Computers— Everyone has at least one good story in them by just telling their own story. Computers make it possible to write and illustrate your story. Share with your family what your early life was like. With your computer you can network throughout the world with America Online, Prodigy, Internet, or CompuServe. To enhance your experience at the computer, refer to Appendix C, *Brain Gym* Activities.

Concert/Symphony— Gather a group of friends together and attend a concert or symphony of your favorite group, singer, or orchestra. Take a class in music appreciation.

Cooking— Now you have time to prepare recipes you've been collecting over the years. This will add variety to those monotonous menus you might have used to save time in meal preparation while you were working. Bake homemade bread or make homemade ice cream. Do you have a special recipe for something that you could enter in cooking or baking contests? Could your product be marketed? Many people have had great marketing success with good family or ethnic recipes. Would you be interested in running a catering business? The Federal Food and Drug Administration, the U.S. Department of Agriculture, and several state agencies  have rules and regulations about food production. Appendix D, Starting a Business, will provide you with some sources of information. Contact a local adult education program or technical college to inquire about taking, or teaching, a cooking class.

Cooking without Fat: Cut the fat in canned goods, soups, stews, and baked beans by placing the can in the refrigerator for thirty minutes before opening. Remove the lid and skim off the solidified fat. This little tip, which also works for homemade soups and stews, is from *Cut the Fat! More Than 500 Easy and*

Enjoyable Ways to Reduce Fat from Every Meal by the American Dietetic Association (Harper Perennial, $7.50).

Food Dictionary: Browse through the Webster's New World Dictionary of Culinary Arts by Sarah Labensky, Gaye Ingram, and Steve Labensky (Prentice Hall, $25.95). Three years of research went into this project.

 Vegetarian Cooking: *Heart Healthy Eating Tips: The Vegetarian Way* describes inexpensive, low fat, high fiber foods and meal choices. Write to the Vegetarian Resource Group, P.O. Box 1463, Baltimore, MD 21203. It's free!

Coupons — Clip coupons. It doesn't take much of your time, and you can save a lot of money. If you've been doing this, you already know of the savings. Go a step further and exchange your unwanted coupons with other coupon clippers. Some supermarkets have special coupon-exchange areas. You'll get even more coupons that are useful to you, and that adds up to more savings! Also, companies often send coupons to customers who call their 800 number.

Crafts — Ideas abound for all kinds of crafts: sewing (dolls, stuffed animals, aprons, quilts, special clothing, to name a few), ceramics, wood-working, tole painting, flower arranging, knitting, crocheting, and many, many more! Crafting is a wonderful way to fill your time and nurture your creativity. Crafts can be sold, entered in craft shows, given as gifts, donated to fund raisers, or entered in various fair competitions for a chance at winning a ribbon. Barb once met a woman who loved to make a particular type of dressed bunny. Each bunny she made was different. She displayed the bunnies at a library and donated proceeds from the sale of her bunnies to buy books for the children's section. What a wonderful and unique idea! She was doing something that she loved and making a special contribution to her community, too. Call 1-800-408-3361 for a free issue and trial subscription to *Handcraft Illustrated*, a magazine filled with crafts and home decorating projects, edited by Carol Endler Sterbenz. Watch your local PBS station or home and garden channel for craft and decorating ideas.

Crime Novels — Read something written by Minette Walters, who not only writes crime novels but also visits criminals in prisons. Her books include *The Ice House, The Sculptress, The Scold's Bridle, The Dark Room,* and *The Echo.* She is fascinated by what has driven somebody to kill another person.

Cults — If you think you or someone you love is being targeted by a cult, contact the Cult Awareness Network at 1-800-556-3055.

Dance, Dance, Dance — It's one of the best ways to improve your social life. A good, smooth dancer is always in demand. Whether the dance is ballroom, Latin, country, or square dancing, it's easy to learn and great fun. If you have a partner, take lessons together. Also try ballet or tap dancing lessons. Dancing single men can become gentlemen-hosts on various cruise lines as dance partners for single ladies who would otherwise not have a dance partner. Check with a travel agent to see which cruise lines use gentlemen-hosts.

Debt — If you are in debt, establish a program to get out of debt. You might choose one of the two sets of guidelines provided here. The first set consists of three general rules.

1. Monthly payments for all debts combined should not exceed more than 40 percent of your pretax income.

2. Divide the price of your car or cars by the number of years you plan to use them. If that amount is more than 10 percent of your gross income, you are spending too much for the car(s).

3. Credit card payments should not exceed 12 percent of your income if you are a single-income family. On more than one income, you can safely have a 15 percent ratio. Credit card payments over 25 percent of your income signal serious trouble.

Here is another set of rules you might choose to follow:

1. Pay yourself first: 10 percent (provides a jingle in your pocket and allows for contingencies).

2. Debt payments should not exceed 20 percent of your after-tax income.

3. Living expenses should not exceed 70 percent of your after-tax income.

Whichever guidelines you choose to follow, the following strategies will help you manage your debt payments:

1. Make the largest payments on debts carrying the lowest interest. (You will pay more of the principal faster, and then you can consolidate the remaining debts with a lower-interest loan).

2. Use debt consolidation loans or home equity loans.

3. If interest rates allow you to refinance your mortgage, you can use the money saved each month to pay off debts.

4. Stop using credit cards.

5. Negotiate payment schedules with credit card companies, or negotiate lower interest rates.

6. If you are in danger of losing your house or car, or your bills are still out of line with what you can pay, downsize or sell your assets.

My main problem is reconciling my gross habits with my net income.

—Errol Flynn

Delta Queen Trip—Take a trip on the Delta Queen or the Mississippi Queen. Live the legend of Mark Twain's Mississippi with a three-to twelve-night trip on an authentic "floating palace." Call for a free brochure, 1-800-543-1949.

Demonstrator—Be a demonstrator in a grocery store.

Depression—Seek professional help in the form of a combination of antidepressant medication and psychiatry, which seem to work well together. For mild cases of depression, sometimes self-care will help. Put a little fun in your life by scheduling something you like to do at least once a week. Get together with others who are cheerful. See a movie, have lunch, play games or cards, have a massage, shop, take a walk. Try other kinds of exercise. Also, try to figure out what's bothering you. Sometimes medications or even food allergies can contribute to depression. The Nutralux Full-Spectrum Light Box might help to improve the way you feel. The cost is approximately $230 each. Call 1-800-705-5559 for information.

Happiness is like a butterfly: the more you chase it, the more it will elude you, but if you turn your attention to other things, it comes and softly sits on your shoulder.

—Robert Lesser

Design — Design a sports arena, stadium, or uniform. Present your plans to the owner of the club or team.

Design Harmony — Learn about Feng Shui (pronounced "fung shway"), an ancient Oriental art of placement of objects and furniture so energy can be balanced or redirected. Books available include *Feng Shui: Harmony by Design* by Nancy SantoPietro (Perigee Books, $15.00) and *Feng Shui Made Easy* by William Spear (Harper San Francisco, $16.00).

Detectors —

Carbon Monoxide Detector: Buy one. Retail stores carry several brands, such as First Alert, American Sensors, Inc., and the new Nighthawk 2000. Low-level exposure to carbon monoxide gas can cause health problems in elderly people and children.

Radon Gas Detector: Check your basement for radon gas, which is the second leading cause of lung cancer in the United States. For more information, call the Environmental Protection Agency (EPA) in your state.

Smoke Detector: Change the battery in your smoke detector each time you adjust your clock for Daylight Saving Time.

Disabilities — Work with people with disabilities. Teach them to play golf or ski. You many want to volunteer with the Special Olympics Program, 1325 G Street NW, Suite 500, Washington, DC 20005 (1-202-628-3630).

Documentary Films — Do you have an idea or the time or the desire to produce a documentary film? As a jumping off point, check with your library reference desk. Also look under *Video* or *Motion Picture Producers and Studios* in the Yellow Pages of a large city phone book.

Dogs—Raise a young puppy to be a Canine Companion for Independence. Puppy raisers begin working with pups that are eight weeks old. You keep them for a year and teach them skills such as stay, sit, come, and an amazing "toilet on command." Call Canine Companions for Independence in your state.

Dog Blood Donors: Check with your local veterinary hospital regarding dog blood transfusions. Veterinarians commonly give blood plasma to dogs with blood clotting problems, severe infections, or anemia, and there is a constant shortage of dog blood. Veterinarian clinics pay as much as $160 a pint for whole dog blood, which is twice the cost of whole human blood. For more information call the Animal Blood Bank in Dixon, California, at 1-916-678-7350.

Dolls—If you collect dolls, you may want to contact Kit Birmingham, who creates beautiful cornhusk dolls and one-of-a-kind dolls sculpted from polymer clay. She specializes in Santas, Mrs. Santas, and character dolls. Write to her at P.O. Box 228, Cedar Crest, NM 87008.

Domestic Violence—Help set up a training program for corporate officials to increase understanding and awareness of domestic violence issues. Work with managers to provide employees concrete suggestions to create a supportive environment for victims. If you are experiencing abuse or you are abusing someone, get help for yourself by calling Social Services. Also, for both men and women, there is a 24-hour Domestic Violence Hot Line; call 1-800-799-7233 for help near you.

Donate—

Donate Your Collections or Valuables: Donate these to a museum, school, or library. Make provisions to pay for the collection's maintenance and growth. Also consider donating property to a worthy cause, organization, or government program. Please be aware that your intentions for the property's use may or may not be carried out.

Donate Musical Instruments: All kinds of musical instruments could be donated to schools, churches, hospitals, nursing homes, and so on. Your generosity may help somebody realize a dream to play music who might never be able to afford the instrument they wish to play. Tricia recently read about a grand piano donated to a hospital and placed in the lobby. It is played by volunteers and walk-ins, professional or amateur, and it brings hours of joy to many people.

Donate Your Organs after Death: For a free brochure on how to donate your organs, write to the Coalition on Donation, P.O. Box 2066, Rock Island, IL 61204-2066. Organs you can donate after death are your heart, kidneys, pancreas, lungs, liver, and intestines. Tissues you can donate include eyes, skin, bone, heart valves, veins, and tendons. The donor's family or estate is never charged.

Draw— Draw poker, or draw pictures or cartoons, or draw up wills, depending on your expertise.

Dreams— Is there something that you've always dreamed of doing? Is it possible to fulfill that dream now?

Driving— Volunteer to drive for those who cannot drive themselves. Call Points of Light at 1-800-59-LIGHT (595-4448). Also consider driving for Meals on Wheels in your area.

I don't want to get to the end of my life and find that I just lived the length of it. I want to have lived the width of it as well.

—Diane Ackerman

E

Eating—For a special treat, make a root beer float or a banana split with chocolate sauce, nuts, and maraschino cherry, topped off with a dab of whipped cream.

Elder Care Home—Open an elder care home. A retired journalist, Bill McBean, found a new calling and opened a couple of elder care homes. He says, "If you had told me five years ago that I would be changing old people's diapers, I would have said you were whacked. But this has made me feel useful for the first time in my life."

Elderhostel—Through this popular program, you can travel to sites throughout the U.S. and Europe, stay at college dorms, and take classes for a very reasonable fee. Write to the National Elderhostel Registration Office, 75 Federal Street, Boston, MA 02110, or call 1-617-426-8056. Spring, summer, and fall/winter catalogs of program offerings are published every year. Visit the Elderhostel home page on the Internet at http://www.elderhostel.org . To request a free service catalog, write Elderhostel, P.O. Box 1959, Department SV, Wakefield, MA 01880 and specifiy service programs.

Engage—Engage anybody and everybody in conversation.

Enter—Enter contests of all kinds.

Estate — Have pity on those who will sort through your house and possessions after you're gone. Sort through any junk now and get rid of it yourself. List collections and valuables — you probably don't want your heirs selling your Heisey Orchid stemware or your priceless jade collection, kachina collection, diamonds, or Oriental rugs for pennies at a garage sale. Make your own funeral and burial arrangements.

Estate Planning — Buy the book *The Complete Book of Trusts* by Martin M. Shenkman, a tax and estate attorney (John Wiley & Sons, $24.95). You can order the book by calling 1-800-225-5945. See your attorney about creating a trust.

Exercise — Start an exercise program, after first consulting your doctor. Regular exercise, whether it be walking, biking, aerobics, swimming, weight training, or other form will give you more energy and a sense of well-being. If you choose an exercise program you enjoy, you'll be more likely to stick to it. Try the Oriental art of tai chi, which is recommended for lowering blood pressure and reducing the risk of falling. Check your library or bookstores for information about tai chi.

Eyeglasses — Collect old eyeglasses in an office building or apartment building near your home by placing a cardboard box in the lobby. When the box is full, contact Medical Ministry International for shipping instructions. The Texas office is P.O. Box 940207, Plano, TX 75094. Their phone number is 1-972-437-1995 and fax number is 1-972-437-1114. The e-mail address is mmitx@computek.net . The Ontario office address is MGM (Canada) Inc., 15 John Street, North, Suite 301, Hamilton, ON L8R 1H1. Their phone number is 905-524-

> **I**ron rusts from disuse, stagnant water loses its purity . . . *even so does inaction sap the vigors of the mind.*
>
> **—Leonardo da Vinci**

3544. You can fax to 905-524-5400, e-mail to vwhz69a@prodigy.com, or visit their website at http://www.mmiusa.org .

Fall Colors— Take trips to see the spectacular fall colors, which are very different in different parts of the country.

Family Memory Book— Start a notebook in which you write what and when your grandchildren say something humorous or heart-touching. You can share these items with your loved ones throughout life.

Fast-Draw Contest— Enter a fast-draw contest. They are usually held in historic towns such as Dodge City, Kansas; Deadwood, South Dakota; Laughlin, Nevada; or Lafayette, Colorado. Fast-draw guns shoot .45 caliber blanks to break balloon targets at 5, 8, 10, 12, and 15 feet. They also hit metal impact targets with wax bullets at 5–15 feet. Timing is by digital readout; electronic fast-draw timers score contestants to a thousandth of a second. The world record is 0.255 second.

Faux Art— This is a method of painting decorations on walls. Learn how to do it, or have it done.

Feel-Good Books— Read a "feel-good" book. Try Jan Karon's "The Mitford Years" series, set in North Carolina. *At Home in Mitford* and

A Light in the Window are two of the titles (Penguin Paperbacks, $11.95 each). A third is *These High Green Hills* (Chariot Victor, $11.95). *Out to Canaan* is newest and in hardcover (Viking, $23.95). All four books are available as audiocassettes.

Festivals — Attend the festivals in your state. Festivals include all kinds of exhibits and activities. They can be focused on music, art, cowboy poetry, quilts, hang gliding, chocolate, auto races and shows, pioneer days, burro days, hot-air balloons, black arts, ice sculptures, kinetic conveyance sculpture races. . . . You're practically guaranteed to enjoy yourself!

Find a Need — And fill it! If you need something, someone else needs it, too. Start looking at what you use every day, even the smallest items. Ask, "What if . . . ? Why not . . . ? What could be improved upon? What little gizmo do I need? If I had arthritis, could I . . . ? If I were in a wheel-chair, could I . . . ?"

Imagination is the highest kite one can fly.

—Lauren Bacall

Fire Safety Video — Get a fire safety video ($19.95) or audiotape ($7.95) by calling 1-800-222-3998. On the Web, visit Fire Safety for Kids, http://www.imall.com/stores/firesafety .

Flooding — Figure out ways to prevent or alleviate flooding. It happens every year with devastating consequences. Should the river beds be dug out? Should higher and stronger dikes be built? Any ideas?

Flower Arranging — Do you have a knack for flower arranging? Florists employ extra help during holidays such as Christmas, Easter, and Mother's Day, and some also use part-time help on a regular basis.

Folk Dancing—Teach others any specialized dances you know, for example, Greek, Russian, Indian, or other dances; or teach folk songs. Offer a class, or volunteer to visit a school or other organization to share your folk knowledge.

Food—Try unusual foods: Moroccan, Algerian, Tunisian, Thai, Japanese, Vietnamese, Ethiopian. Prepare dishes yourself, or visit  an ethnic restaurant. Listen to recordings on the safest way to cook, serve, store, and travel with food. Weekdays, get advice from an expert live on the USDA Meat and Poultry Hotline at 1-800-535-4555.

Foreign Languages—Learn a foreign language. Maybe you plan to travel, and learning another language would make your trip more enjoyable. Translators are always needed in the medical field, as well as in the business world and in government. Read the book *How to Learn Any Language* by Barry Farber (Citadel Press, $10.95). Farber is the founder of The Language Club, 600 Madison Avenue, New York, NY 10022 (1-800-447-2665). "Foreign Languages for Travelers" teaches a basic travel vocabulary for more than forty languages. The website is http://www.travlang.com/languages .

Fraud—Complain about "lousy products, flimsy warranties, and bad service." Get the book *Consumer Terrorism* by Elinor Burkett and Frank Bruni (Harper Perennial, $12.00). This book lists state-by-state consumer protection offices and describes how to complain for best results in consumer fraud cases.

Friends—Friends will take on a whole new meaning. Retirement can be dull with no one else around. If you're the only one at home on your block during the day, you'll have to scout around for a buddy to do things with. Sociability is really necessary now. If you have several buddies, you can help each other with projects. For instance, you help Bob with a brake job on his car, then both of you help Joe cut and split wood for his fireplace, and then both Joe and Bob help you paint your house. Next week, you and your significant other can go to Bob's mountain retreat with his significant other to help paint the decks and stairways, play miniature golf, have a nice dinner, spend the night, and enjoy the mountains. The week after that you can help Joe hang the new chandelier in the dining room of his daughter's house, and then eat the fresh trout you, Joe, and his son-in-law catch in the afternoon. Retirement can be a big round of receiving and returning favors, to the advantage and enjoyment of everyone concerned.

True happiness is of a retired nature, and an enemy to pomp and noise; it arises, in the first place, from the enjoyment of one's self; and in the next, from the friendship and conversation of a few select companions.

—Joseph Addison

Games—Play some of the games people used to play: Authors, Scrabble, dominoes, cribbage, checkers, pinochle, jacks, pick-up-sticks. Consider creating new games. Have a few friends over and enjoy a game of bocce ball, ping pong, pool, or croquet.

Gangster-Style, Murder Mystery Dinner Party—Host your own "How to Host a Murder" dinner party with each of your guests acting out a part. (Each game comes in a box, and there are different themes.)

You can make this as realistic as you want by sending out invitations and assigning each guest a role to play, complete with people wearing costumes to suit their parts, or the party can be very casual and impromptu. The instructions are easy to follow, and the game is a *lot* of fun. There are a variety of murder mysteries to solve, available wherever games are sold.

Zest is the secret of all beauty. There is no beauty that is attractive without zest.

—Christian Dior

Garage Sales—Garage sales are a great way to make money, have fun, and meet people. Make sure you have plenty of stuff priced in the nickel and dime range. Be willing to dicker on prices. Make waterproof, easy-to-read signs, and post them on busy streets, pointing in the right direction. Open early in the morning, by seven or eight o'clock, depending on your area. If you wait much later to open, you will have missed about two hundred early-bird buyers. Also, you might want to do "estate sales," where you go in and price everything in the house of a deceased or elderly person, sell what you can, give 75 percent of the proceeds to the relatives, and pocket the other 25 percent. Then you haul away whatever is not wanted or sold, FREE.

Gardening—Maybe you've never had time to have a garden because of your job. Now you can indulge in either a small or a large garden, or maybe change some of your landscaping. Organic gardening is really catching on, and people are looking to buy produce that has not been contaminated with pesticides. Ask the County Extension Service to recommend plants and flowers that attract butterflies and hummingbirds; flower and shade plants that will grow in the shade of your mature trees; or ornamental grasses for your yard. If you don't have space for a garden, contact the County Extension Service—they sometimes offer seniors a ten-foot-square plot for gardening. Does becoming a Master Gardener sound appealing? If so, inquire at the

Extension Service, a local botanical garden, or a college in your area for more information.

Extra Produce?: Donate your extra produce to the hungry. Contact your place of worship, homes for battered women, rescue missions, or a community food ministry; or call Second Harvest, a nationwide network of food banks (1-312-263-2303), or Food Chain (1-800-345-3009). If you plant long-keeping root vegetables, such as onions, leeks, carrots, potatoes, and parsnips, these make great winter soups.

Gardening Books: Garden to your heart's content with the new book *The Twenty-Minute Gardener: The Garden of Your Dreams without Giving Up Your Life, Your Job, or Your Sanity* by Martin Asher (Random House, $19.95). Obtain *The Complete Kitchen Garden* by Patrick Bowe (Macmillan, $35.00), which features glorious gardens of England, France, and North America, in which vegetables, flowers, and fruit-bearing plants are arranged in a variety of new ways.

Gardening in Containers: Consider buying a self-watering container system called Living Tapestries, the Fence That Grows. It is a set of interconnecting panels that can be planted with everything from petunias to peppers. The growing medium is sphagnum moss, which increases humidity and lessens frost damage.

Gourmet Garden Tools: Check out Smith & Hawken (1-800-776-3336) at Two Arbor Lane, Florence, KY 41022-6900. Visit the Williams-Sonoma stores. Request a catalog from Gardeners Eden (1-800-822-9600), which carries fancy, expensive European garden tools that are made well and will last a long time.

Internet websites for gardeners:

Gardening on the Web
http://www.gardening.com

The NoProblem Garden
　　　http://www.netusal.net/~lindley/
WebGarden FactSheet Database
　　　http://hortwww-2.ag.ohio-state.edu
GardenNet
　　　http://www.trine.com/GardenNet/

To watch the corn grow, or the blossoms set; to draw hard breath over the ploughshare or spade; to read, to think, to love, to pray, are the things that make men happy.

—John Ruskin

Garlic—Enter the Great Gilroy Garlic Recipe Contest and Cook-Off. For contest rules and dates, send a self-addressed, stamped envelope to Gilroy Garlic Festival Association, P.O. Box 2311, Gilroy, CA 95021.

Genealogy—Create or expand the record of your family tree. If you're not sure how to go about doing this, community colleges offer genealogy courses to help you get started. Then share your results with other members of your family. Find your great-grandparents' birthplaces through the Internet on the Social Security Death Index, hosted by the genealogy site Ancestry. You can also check the Social Security Administration's records of deceased social security numbers. Go to the website http://www.ancestry.com/ssdi/ .

Every generation revolts against its fathers and makes friends with its grandfathers.

—Lewis Mumford

Get Out of the House—For a little while every day, leave your residence, if only to walk around the shopping mall, visit with the neighbors, or enjoy a sack lunch at the park. The sociability of other people is important to emotional health.

Gift for Mom—As a special gift for Mom, send $100 to the National Women's Hall of Fame. Mom will be named to the national institution's Wall of Fame: Her name will be inscribed on a plaque and displayed on a wall in the institution in Seneca Falls, New York. A replica of the plaque will be mailed to you. Call 1-315-568-8060.

"Give Back"—Give back to society what it has given to you. A New York designer, Norma Kamali, went back to her high school and helped art students start their own T-shirt business. She persuaded Canon to loan a color copier and printer, and Anvil, a T-shirt company, to donate the first 250 T-shirts and to give a discount on future purchases. A contest for the design was won by Prince Neufville, whose design incorporates "the two things most important to kids—radios and boots." Profits will be shared 50/50 by the students and the school. Contact Kamali's OMO shop, 11 West Fifty-sixth Street, New York, NY 10019. Do you have a talent you could use to help someone reach their potential?

Gluten-Free—If you need wheat-free, gluten-free mixes for cooking or baking, write to Ener-G Foods, Inc., P.O. Box 84487, Seattle, WA 98124-4787. Quinoa Corporation makes a wheat-free, gluten-free pasta. Their address is P.O. Box 1039, Torrance, CA 90505. The Gluten-Free Pantry, a Connecticut-based mail-order company, sells fifteen gluten-free mixes for brownies, pasta, muffins, bagels, breads, and more. Their address is P.O. Box 881, Glastonbury, CT 06033-0881. The phone number is 1-860-633-3826.

Goals—Buy the book *Unlimit Your Life: Setting and Getting Goals* by James Fadiman, Ph.D. (Celestial Arts Publishing Co., $12.95). The book tells how to move beyond a vague idea about what you want to be different in your life. It explains how to move past internal barriers and low self-esteem, how to decide if a goal is truly what you want or only what someone else wants for you, and finally how to achieve your goal.

Gold Panning/Prospecting—Do you live in an area where gold mining is a part of its history? If so, you'll probably still find people out panning for gold. Consider joining a group that plans regular gold-panning activities.

Golf—Golf is great fun, as well as great frustration. Join a golf league and play once or twice a week. You'll meet lots of nice people. On the Internet, visit the website GolfWeb (http://www.golfweb.com/). To improve your game, watch golf videos, which can be obtained from the library. Watch golf tournaments on television. Take lessons from a golf pro at your club. Order *Switched on Golf* by Pamela Curlee (Edu-K Foundation, $35.00; call 1-805-650-3303 to get this manual of brain exercises designed to improve your game; a video is planned for the future). Golf courses are some of the most beautiful places on earth, and you'll be walking on grass you didn't have to mow, water, or trim. (Golf courses are so beautiful because large amounts of pesticides are used in their maintenance, so don't put golf tees or balls in your mouth and don't walk a course barefoot or in sandals. Wash your hands when you get off the course.) Ping golf clubs were made by Karsten Solheim because he didn't like the ready-made golf clubs; build your own golf clubs in your garage—try the Golf Works at 1-800-848-8358, or fax 1-800-800-3290.

Government Contracts—For doing business with the government, you may need help on proposal preparation, contract negotiation, government accounting, subcontracting, policies, procedures and contract administration. Contact D.L. Larsen Associates, P.O. Box 280601, Lakewood, CO 80228-0601. Call them at 1-303-275-9923, or

fax 1-303-275-9926. This firm specializes in environmental and cost reimbursement contracts. Different firms will have different specialties.

Graphoanalysis — Learn how to read people's personality and character traits in their handwriting. Contact the International Graphoanalysis Society, 111 North Canal Street, Chicago, IL 60606, or call 1-312-930-9446.

Greeter — Be a greeter at your local Wal-Mart store.

Grieving — Try not to grieve too much over friends and loved ones who have divorced, moved away, or died. Concentrate on the good times you had together. Always part as friends so that you will have no regrets if you don't meet again. As the Russian poet Pushkin said, "Never say with grief, 'He is no more,' but rather say with thankfulness, 'He was.'"

Grooming — This continues to be important even in retirement. What if someone calls and wants to go to lunch in thirty minutes? You don't want to decline because you look frumpy or disheveled. If no one calls, you call them. Also, you don't have to look or act old or dirty. Keep your hair trimmed and colored, if you like. Your nails and clothing should be neat and clean. An old friend of Tricia's would look down on his soiled shirt and say, "I used to hate dirty old men and darned if I didn't become one." It's not necessary to spend a lot of money on clothes, either. Goodwill thrift stores and consignment shops often have brand-new or near-new items. You just need to look carefully. You can also find nice clothing at garage sales.

Style is primarily a matter of instinct.

—Bill Blass

H

Habitat for Humanity — Volunteer to help build a home with Habitat for Humanity, which is now building "green," which means they use energy-efficient and environmentally friendly construction techniques. Special skills are not required; anyone can help. Call 1-800-HABITAT (422-4828).

Hair — Do you have a knack for working with hair? If you do, this can be an idea for a small, part-time business, or you may find doing haircare for people in nursing homes a rewarding experience. Learn how to french-braid hair. Have a computer imaging service show you how you would look with different hair styles.

Harmonica — Learn how to play a harmonica. For a beginner's guide, send a self-addressed, stamped envelope (#10 size) to: Hohner, Inc., P.O. Box 15035, Richmond, VA 23227-5035.

Harmony — Have you noticed that nobody seems to know how to harmonize anymore? Teach or learn two-, three-, or four-part harmony. Sing for yourself or to entertain others.

 Health Club or YMCA — Consider joining a health club to aid your physical and cardiovascular well-being. It's also another place to meet people.

Health Newsletter — Get Wellness Letter, an informative newsletter on preventive medicine, written by the University of California at Berkeley. If costs $15 for a one-year trial subscription. Contact to order: Wellness Letter, P.O. Box 420148, Palm Coast, FL 32142 or http://www.enews.com/magazines/ucbwl . Johns Hopkins Hospital publishes a medical newsletter entitled "Health after 50." Write to P.O. Box 420176, Palm Coast, FL 32142.

Healthy Eating — Eat a diet rich in fruits, vegetables, and low-fat dairy products to reduce your blood pressure, the risk of heart disease, and the likelihood of stroke.

Hearing — Send for the booklet *Communicating with People Who Have a Hearing Loss* from the Alexander Graham Bell Association for the Deaf, 3417 Volta Place, NW, Washington, DC 20007. The first copy is free. If you want to order in bulk, you can buy ten copies for $3.00, fifty copies for $11.50, and one hundred copies for $20.00.

Hearing Dogs — Whether you need a hearing dog or you want to train hearing dogs, contact International Hearing Dogs, Inc., at 5901 East 89th Avenue, Henderson, CO 80640 (1-303-287-3277).

Heart Disease — Get a heart disease risk assessment quiz, walking tapes, and low-salt cookbook from the American Heart Association, 1-800-AHA-USA1 (242-8721) or on the Web at http://www.amhrt.org/index.html . The cost is $5.99.

Help Young People To Be Creative — Get them away from the television. Children need to be doers to develop a sense of appreciation

Imagination is more important than knowledge.

—Albert Einstein

of themselves and others. Give them paper, pencils, crayons, paints, or clay, and let their imagination create the lines and mix the colors. If they are interested in music, buy them an instrument and help them stay motivated to practice.

Heritage— Heritage is your family history. Look back and see if there is something from the old country that people in the U.S. might enjoy.

Hiking— Many hundreds of trails exist in our country and beyond. Some of the trails are probably much closer than you realize. Hiking is wonderful exercise, and it allows you to experience parts of the world that only those willing to engage in these excursions will see. Hiking also allows excellent time for reflection. Read *Hiking! The Ultimate Natural Prescription for Health and Wellness* by Philip Ferranti and Cecelia Layva with Joie Goodkin (Kendall/Hunt Publishing, $14.95). The book contains tips on conditioning yourself, dressing properly, selecting appropriate routes, staying safe on the trail, and planning for changes in weather. It also tells you how to find hiking clubs with members whose skills and interests will be compatible with yours. See Appendix E, Travel Tips, for further information.

HMO Comparison— Contact the National Committee for Quality Assurance (NCQA) to find out how your HMO (health maintenance organization) compares with others. You can get a detailed report card on most HMOs. For a free report call 1-800-839-6487 or visit http://www.ncqa.org .

Hokey— Do the hokey pokey, bunny hop, chicken dance, conga line, or hucklebuck.

Holiday Pageants — Work with others at your place of worship to stage a play depicting an important event or turning point in the history of your religion. An increasingly popular type of pageant creates "living pictures," a series of tableaus formed by actors, including children, posing in different scenes. The house lights are dimmed and the actors re-pose themselves between scenes. Each scene may be accompanied by narration, delivered either by a narrator or by the actors themselves.

Holidays — Relish your favorite holidays more than ever: Valentine's Day, Independence Day, Oktoberfest, Thanksgiving, Hanukkah, Christmas, Kwanzaa, and so on. Share with your family or friends some of the traditional holiday activities your ancestors delighted in. Enjoy baking, sing-a-longs, sleigh rides, handmade decorations, and homemade cards, candies, and gifts.

Home Maintenance — Have your lawn mowed, windows washed, or snow shoveled in a timely fashion.

Hospice — This is a fairly new concept in America and might be a good business opportunity. Father Paul von Lobkowitz, age sixty-four, started the Hospice of St. John in Lakewood, Colorado, with only "ten cents and a can of paint" in 1976. The hospice serves terminally ill patients; the average length of stay is about twelve days.

Hot-Air Balloon — Take a hot-air balloon, glider, or skydiving ride for some special occasion. Attend hot-air balloon races or shows. These are especially popular in the Southwest.

House-Sit — House-sit for friends or other people while they go on vacation.

How Do You View Retirement?—Do you look at retirement as an opportunity to do things you've always wanted to do but never had time for, or as the beginning of the end? Some people go home, twiddle their thumbs, and die within months after retirement. *Don't let this happen to you!* Reread the Introduction and then pick at least two activities to do within the next month. Don't forget to skim the "Let Your Imagination Soar" activities, too, for ideas.

> The most wasted day of all is that on which we have not laughed.
>
> —Nicolas Chamfort

Humor—"Humor greases the skids of life." Enjoy a good laugh every day. Find humor in tense situations. Read books by Bill Cosby, Dave Barry, and Erma Bombeck. Enjoy the book *Compassionate Laughter: Jest for Your Health* by Patty Wooten (Commune-A-Key, $12.95). Visit an Internet site for humor. Choices include the American Association for Therapeutic Humor (http://www.callamer.com/itc/aath); Patty Wooten's website (http://www.mother.com/jesthome); and Touchstar Productions, which offers audio and video tapes as well as educational materials (http://www.touchstarpro.com).

I Remember Mama—Start an "I Remember Mama" brunch to honor elderly women who might be alone on Mother's Day.

Ice Fishing—Go ice fishing and take along a couple of buddies.

Ideas — Ideas are fleeting. Keep a scrap of paper or a notebook handy to jot down your ideas before they're gone.

Identify Your Identity — Just what is your identity? Are you Joe(sephine) Blow, Vice President of Marketing of Higgeldy Piggeldy Stores; or Joe(sephine) Blow, Little League coach, watercolorist, formidable chess player, and champion bass fisher? If your entire identity is in the corporate title you once held or in a corporate structure, you might want to open a business; be a consultant; get on the board of a bank, zoo, or fraternal organization; run for political office; or campaign for a political candidate. Consider joining the Senior Corps of Retired Executives (SCORE); for information on SCORE, contact the Small Business Administration in your town, or the U.S. Small Business Administration at 1441 L Street, Washington, DC 20416; website http://www.score.org .

Immigrants — Especially if you are proficient in a foreign language, you can help immigrants prepare for the citizenship test and interview. Contact your place of worship or the U.S. Immigration and Naturalization Service listed in the Federal Government section of your phone book.

Improvisation — Enjoy improvisational comedy. Take or teach a class. Visit or perform in a comedy club.

Income Tax — Preparing income tax return forms for elderly people might prove an interesting and rewarding service.

Indoors or Outdoors — Where do you enjoy being? You decide, and then pick appropriate activities.

Insurance—Inventory the contents of your home by photographing or videotaping your possessions, and then keep this record of your belongings in a safe deposit box. You'll be prepared if disaster strikes, and your insurance company will be more inclined to give you a fair settlement. Shop around for the best prices for homeowner's insurance. AARP insurance is reasonable, especially if you insure your home and cars. Also, check out nursing home insurance for future coverage needs.

Internet for Seniors—Following are several interesting Internet sites specifically intended for seniors.

GoldenAge.Net: Resources for seniors and their caregivers.
http://elo.mediasrv.swt.edu/goldenage/script.html

Goldngal: Hosted by Kathleen Gallagher, who started Internet Relay Chat (IRC) Channel 65 Plus. Many age groups chat about everything.
http://www.fyi.net/~goldngal/goldn2.htm

National Senior Service Corps: National volunteer service program for people aged fifty-five and older.
http://www.cns.gov/senior-a.html

The Resource Directory for Older People: A directory of government agencies and resource centers on aging.
http://www.aoa.dhhs.gov/aoa/resource.html

SeniorNet: An international community of computer-using seniors with forums on America Online (keyword: seniors) and the Microsoft Network. SeniorNet is a not-for-profit network based in San Francisco; nationwide it supports more than one hundred community learning centers where those fifty-five and older can learn about computers. More than 90,000 people have mastered their home computers through SeniorNet.

• •

There is a special Generation to Generation area where seniors can mentor students of all ages. Also, once you are in this website, you can click on "Sharing Memories" to find thousands of postings on World War II, and seniors can visit with students about the war.

http://www.seniornet.org

Seniors On-Line Age of Reason: Supersite with 5,000 cyberlinks for those fifty years and older.

http://www.ageofreason.com/

World War II—Keeping the Memory Alive: An archive and message board for WWII veterans and their families. Patricia Farley, who served in the Women's Royal Naval Service (Wrens), has posted her complete WWII memoirs here.

http://www.pagesz.net/~jbdavis/ww2.html

Consumer Network: This is not specifically for seniors, but you might be interested in product research.

http://www.consumerworld.org/

Invention Fair—Attend Invention Fairs, which are held worldwide. On the Internet, use a search engine such as AltaVista or Yahoo. There are thousands of listings.

Investing—Reevaluate your investments upon retirement. Learn what investments are good for retirees. After all, you've worked all these years to save for your retirement, so make it enjoyable and lasting. Community colleges offer investment courses, and investment companies offer informative seminars.

Irish Dancing—If you enjoy Irish dancing, order the Riverdance video; call 1-800-811-8802.

Islamic Clothing—Here's another "find a need and fill it" idea. Entrepreneur Umm Zamzam was unable to find authentic Islamic clothing to wear, so she now sells it through her business, Caravan Xpress, at 1-757-440-0441.

Jackie—Organize a Camelot-era party where people come in "White House cocktail attire" and donate a fee for some worthy cause. Have a contest for Jackie look-a-likes to serve as hostesses for the party. Ladies who dress Jackie-style (short dress, pearls, and a pillbox hat) get in free. Decorate in red, white, and blue, and have a great time.

Japan—We found the following information interesting and wanted to share it with you. Let it form the basis of a conversation with a friend or family member. The excerpt is from an article written by Joe Volz for *Maturity News Service*.

> Japan has more than 35% of those over the age of 65 still working, compared to only 16% in the United States. Another interesting comparison, compiled by Dr. Joseph Flaherty of the St. Louis University School of Medicine, is that only 7% of older Japanese live alone, compared to nearly 40% in this country. "Many people point to the Japanese respect for elders and say we need more of that here in the U.S.," says Flaherty. He says parents living with their children can be a plus. Being around the grandchildren and having a sense of purpose in

the household can improve the quality of life. But he also found that this dependence results in a loss of independent thinking, a value highly esteemed in the United States. Flaherty notes that dependence in Japan means financial dependence. Older adults in Japan receive almost 25% of their living expenses from their children. Older adults in the U.S. receive less than 3%.

Join a League—Join a league to bowl, to play baseball, to golf, or whatever. You will have something to look forward to at least one day each week.

Karaoke—Enjoy singing in a karaoke night spot.

Kites—Kite flying is an inexpensive family activity that provides endless hours of fun. For more information, contact Into the Wind, 1408 Pearl St., Boulder, CO 80302 (1-800-541-0314). Their fax number is 1-303-449-7315, and the e-mail address is kites@intothewind.com . Visit their website at http://www.intothewind.com .

Knees—Read *Save Your Knees* by James M. Fox, M.D., an orthopedic surgeon (Dell Publishing Co., $8.95). The book discusses major causes of injury; prevention methods; ways to build strength in the muscle groups surrounding the knee joints; specific exercises; and rehabilitation.

K'NEX—It's the name of a construction toy set (colored pieces of plastic that snap together anywhere along the length of the rod) created by Joel Glickman. Buy this for your grandchildren, or tell them to ask Santa for it. K'NEX is available at toy stores nationwide.

Korean Finger Math—This is something you or your grandchildren might want to learn because it enables you to do large sums by counting on your fingers. Buy *The Complete Book of Finger Math* by Edwin M. Lieberthal (McGraw-Hill, $22.00).

Landscaping—By the highways through town, the landscaping may start out as grass but always turns to weeds. Come up with a better idea utilizing xeriscape (a science using drought-resistant plants in landscaping, very popular in arid parts of the country). Check with your local extension service for plants that grow well in your area, be it wet or dry.

Large Sizes—Large-size goods for men, women, and children can be ordered from the *Royal Resources Directory* (Vendredi Enterprises, $29.95). It covers art to wigs and everything in between. A separate shoe and clothing directory is available for $12. Call Vendredi Enterprises at 1-408-739-4192, or write to P.O. Box 220, Camas Valley, OR 97416-0220. To receive the Amplestuff catalog, call 1-914-679-3316 or write P.O. Box 116, Bearsville, NY 12409. The address for the National Association to Advance Fat Acceptance is P.O. Box 188620, Sacramento, CA 95818. Their phone is 1-916-558-6880, and the website is http://www.naafa.org .

Laser—Raise funds to implement the use of lasers to remove tattoos from kids who no longer wish to belong to a gang.

Legal Services Made Affordable—If you don't already have a will or trust, now would be a good time to take care of this. Statistics show that 70 percent of all Americans do not have a will. Pre-Paid Legal Services, Inc., and subsidiaries make access to legal services very affordable to members. Legal service plans are available for individuals, families, small businesses, and groups. For a small monthly membership fee ($25.00 for the expanded family plan), members receive benefits under five (in most states) areas of coverage. Your membership includes preparation of a standard will, with annual updates, by an attorney. The Pre-Paid Legal Services plan enables you and your family to practice *preventive* law. Other coverage

Riches are not from an abundance of wordly goods, but from a contented mind.

—Mohammed

includes unlimited telephone consultation, phone calls or letters on your behalf, contract and document review, moving traffic ticket and other motor vehicle legal services, trial defense for civil and job-related criminal charges, IRS audit legal services, and a discounted fee for services that do not fall under title coverage. For more information or a membership application, write to your independent associate at 10307 West 58th Place, Arvada, CO 80004. (Note: The above is not intended to be a complete description of benefits. Consult a membership contract for a complete description of plan benefits and exclusions.)

History: Pre-Paid Legal Services, Inc., was founded by Mr. Harland Stonecipher in 1972. Mr. Stonecipher was involved in a car accident and was sued even though he wasn't at fault. He realized he had medical insurance to cover his medical expenses and car insurance to cover his car repair expenses, but he had nothing to help cover the cost of defending himself in the lawsuit. There is nothing to stop someone from suing you. This type of service has been available in Europe since the 1930s and is as important there as car insurance and medical insurance. You wouldn't dream of going without medical or car insurance, and yet almost no one insures themselves against legal situations that can be just as financially devastating as a serious illness or car accident.

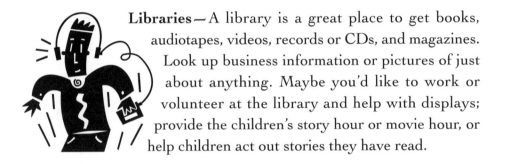

Libraries—A library is a great place to get books, audiotapes, videos, records or CDs, and magazines. Look up business information or pictures of just about anything. Maybe you'd like to work or volunteer at the library and help with displays; provide the children's story hour or movie hour, or help children act out stories they have read.

Long Term Care—If you have an aging parent, partner, or live-alone friend, discuss long term care with them by stressing how planning now will help them retain control over what happens to them later. For example, how important is it to stay in their own home if the time comes when they can no longer care for themselves? How will they prefer to obtain meals if they can no longer cook? Record their answers for future reference, and share the information with other friends or family members so that everyone will know the aging person's preferences to avoid conflicts in carrying them out.

An elegant sufficiency, content, retirement, rural quiet, friendship, books.

—James Thomson

M

Makeover — Have a makeover done or a glamour picture taken. Watch what the stylist does so that you can repeat the makeover at home. If you won't be able to see because they take off your glasses, bring a friend with you and then you can practice on each other. Have a head-to-toe makeover — hairdo, face, clothing. Wearing your best colors will improve your appearance and morale. If you don't know what colors look good on you, get the book *Color Me Beautiful* by Carole Jackson (Ballantine Books, Inc., $15.00), or check your local Yellow Pages under *Color Consultants* for a personal color consultation.

Mammogram — Retirement-aged women are well-advised to have a yearly mammogram and gynecological exam. If you're about due or overdue, make the appointment now.

Massage — Get a body massage. Learn to massage your significant other. Try Shiatsu.

Maternity Exercise Outfits — If you know someone who is expecting, share this information with her. Designer Sharon Wolf Doyle, a fitness fanatic and instructor, got pregnant. She found that there were no workout clothes for pregnant women on the market. She "found a need and filled it." She began designing, manufacturing, and selling exercise garments for pregnant women. Her Wolf Wear is a home-based business in Lafayette, Colorado. The phone number is 1-303-665-8980.

Maze— Try finding your way out of a human maze. Stand up on top and cheer on someone else as they try to find their way out. A human maze is much like an animal maze, because once you enter you are searching for a way out. The human mazes Tricia has seen are made of wood, approximately 40 x 60 feet, open to the sky (no roof), and consisting of hallways and doorways, many leading to dead ends. A person enters and goes up and down the hallways, into every little cubbyhole, looking for the way out. Usually, the person is given a piece of paper or a card and gets it stamped with a rubber stamp at various checkpoints in the maze. There is a stairway on the outside that leads to an observation deck that looks down on the participants ("victims") trying to get out. You can cheer, help, or hinder them in their travels.

Medical Supplies for Homecare— Here's another "find a need and fill it" idea. Two sisters, Mary and Patricia Curry, started a home medical supply company after caring for their father. You can order all necessary supplies from CurryCare, 1-800-720-7440, or P.O. Box 2448, Cupertino, CA 95015-2448.

> **G**od created memory so that we might have roses in December.
>
> —Italo Svevo

Memory— Everyone age thirty-five and over has memory lapses. You find yourself in the middle of a room wondering where you were headed and why, or you suddenly draw a blank on what you were about to say, or you can't connect a name with a face. Don't fret. You're probably just distracted, or your memory banks are overloaded. Dr. Daniel L. Alkon, a scientist at the National Institute of Health, has written a paperback titled *Memory's Voice* (Harper Collins Publishers, Inc., $22.50). Just a little note: To help yourself concentrate on remembering something, write it down in very small handwriting. Please also refer to *Brain Gym* Activities (Appendix C) as they may enhance your memory.

"Mending Fences"—If mending fences, or making amends, is important to you, try to resolve any continuing differences with family members or friends. The little (or big) walls we build over things—things we sometimes don't even remember—can rob us of a great deal of gladness in life.

Kind words can be short and easy to speak, but their echoes are truly endless.

—Mother Teresa

Menopause—If you are going through menopause, treatment doesn't have to include hormones. Hormone replacement therapy is one choice; natural alternatives for symptoms are another choice. You should decide only after consulting with your doctor and becoming informed about the pros and cons of both types of treatment. Send for the free booklet *Managing Menopause: What to Expect, How to Ease the Transition,* provided by the National Institute on Aging, Information Center, Box 8057, Gaithersburg, MD 20898-8057, or call 1-800-222-2225.

Mental or Scholastic Interests Can Be Pursued—A neighbor of Tricia's holds seventeen United States Patent Office patents. He has never sold anything from them, but he enjoys the mental gymnastics that lead up to applying for and obtaining those patents. It's all he talks about. He has his creative juices going full blast all day every day.

The mind of the people is like mud, from which arise strange and beautiful things.

—W. J. Turner

Metric System—Find a way to promote the metric system in the United States. Don't tell people to get out their conversion tables; that hasn't worked. Maybe if you could replace every yardstick with a meterstick . . . ?

Miracles—Read *A Course in Miracles* (Foundation for Inner Peace, $40.00). Join a study/support group for whatever's bothering you. Buy a set of *Little Miracles*™ cards (Compendium, Inc., $4.95; call 1-800-914-3327). Each card measures about 2" x 2.5" and has a reassuring or thought-provoking quotation inside. You can write a note on the back under the words "Expect a Miracle" and include it in a letter to a friend.

> **J**oy is a net of love by which you can catch souls.
>
> —Mother Teresa

Missionary — Become a missionary or consider some other vocation through your place of worship.

Model — Be a model or an actor or extra in movies made locally. Directors and producers are always looking for mature, suave, debonair people.

> **T**hey told me to fix my teeth, change my nose, even get out of the business. But I stayed, and learned, and didn't give up.
>
> —Lauren Hutton

Model Railroads — Build/buy/sell/trade trains and layouts.

Moles — Have your moles checked, especially if any of the following conditions exist: (1) The mole is asymmetrical or irregularly shaped. (2) The border is jagged or blurry-looking. (3) The color is getting darker or changing. (4) The diameter is more than one-fourth inch. (5) The mole is uneven or elevated. To obtain a free brochure on spotting and preventing skin cancer, courtesy of the American Academy of Family Physicians, send your request with a self-addressed, business-sized, stamped envelope to Skin Cancer, c/o AAFP, P.O. Box 19326, Lenexa, KS 66285.

Motorhome — Get in your motorhome and see the country! You can join the fun, fellowship, and activities of fellow RV'ers (recreational vehicle users). Good Sam Club and Escapees, Inc., are motorhome (RV) clubs with wonderful benefits for their members. Benefits and services include discounts on camping fees, emergency road service, auto and RV insurance plans, medical and hospital insurance plans, trip-routing services, mail forwarding services, lost key and lost pet services, American Express travelers checks, and many, many others. For more information contact the clubs:

Escapees, Inc.
100 Rainbow Drive
Livingston, TX 77351
　　Phone: 1-409-327-8873

Good Sam Club
P.O. Box 6888
Englewood, CO 80155
　　Phone: 1-800-234-3450
　　Website: http://www.roads.tl.com

Wally Byam Caravan Club International (WBCCI)
803 East Pike Street
Jackson Center, OH 45334
　　Phone: 1-937-596-5211
　　Website: http://www.channel1.com/wbcci

Moving— Moving is a big decision. Do you want to move to a retirement community with underground secured parking, organized activities, swimming pool, golf, and tennis? Do you want assisted living services or an onsite health care center? Do you want to stay where you are?

 Multiple Sclerosis— If you or someone you know has multiple sclerosis, and you want outdoor experiences and confidence-building challenges, contact Charlotte Robinson at Adventures Within, 1250 Ogden Street, Denver, CO 80210, or visit the National Multiple Sclerosis Society website at http://www.nmss.org .

Music — Music is important to your mental health. Play music you enjoy listening to. Are you sick and tired of "moldy oldies" that remind you of high school? Country music is popular and fairly easy on the nerves. But does it say what you really want to hear? Write a song about how you feel right now; what you're going through right now; what you're happy or sad about. George Weidler, a policeman in Federal Heights, Colorado, writes songs using a tape recorder while in his patrol car. He wrote a tearjerker titled "Who'll Find the Children?" about missing children. He has been recognized by Find the Children, a nonprofit organization in Los Angeles, which is using Weidler's creation as its theme song.

Music Festivals — Attend music festivals from Mozart to jazz. Check the Entertainment section of your local newspaper.

My advice is don't spend money on therapy. Spend it in a record store.

—Wim Wenders

Needlecrafts — Try knitting, crocheting, embroidery, or needlepoint; all are fun and easy to learn.

New York Public Library Telephone Reference Service — These wonderful people can answer almost any question in just a few minutes. They have countless encyclopedias, almanacs, and dictionaries, including volumes on trademarks, inventions, coins, holidays, temperature and heat-wave records, whatever interests you. Call 1-212-340-0849 Monday through Friday, 9:00 A.M. to 6:00 P.M. (Eastern standard time).

Newseum — Visit the Newseum in Arlington, Virginia, a $50 million, multimedia monument to the world of news. There you can write your own news story or be videotaped reading a report in front of a backdrop of the White House; you can give the weather or be a play-by-play sports announcer. Tapes are approximately $15. You can also check what the news of the day was on the day you were born.

Newspaper — Read the newspaper for ideas of things to do, buy, or sell. Do the crossword and other puzzles. Read the funnies.

Numerology — Have your numbers done. It's interesting and great fun. Write to Numerology Profile, One Comac Loop, Suite 14, Ronkonkoma, NY 11779.

Nursing Home Pets — Contact your local Humane Society and ask about taking dogs and kittens into nursing homes to boost residents' morale during visits. Read *Life Worth Living* by Dr. William Thomas, an award-winning book about a program called the Eden Alternative, which uses animals, plants, and children to fight the plagues of loneliness, helplessness, and boredom in elderly persons (VanderWyk & Burnham, $17.95).

Open Houses—Hold an open house for any special occasion. Go to realtors' open houses and see how other homes are decorated.

Orienteering—Learn to use a compass to find your way around. U.S. Orienteering information is available from Silva Orienteering Service/USA, P.O. Box 1604, Binghamton, NY 13902. Read the updated version of Bjorn Kjellstrom's 1955 classic *Be Expert with Map and Compass: The Complete Orienteering Handbook* (Macmillan Publishing Co., Inc., $17.00). Orienteering classes are sometimes available at local

outdoor sporting goods stores such as REI (Recreational Equipment, Inc.; 1-800-426-4840).

Osteoporosis—Fight osteoporosis through exercise, such as walking, dancing, and weight training. Get your doctor's advice before starting the exercise program. If you are taking Fosamax, take it with *warm* water.

One can never creep when one feels an impulse to soar.

—Helen Keller

P

Pain—See your doctor. Consider hypnosis, acupuncture, massage therapy, herbal therapy, or other alternative medicine. See also the entry "Relax."

Paint and Brighten Up Your Home with Color—A fresh coat of paint and some colorful accessories will do wonders for your home. *Color: A Stroke of Brilliance,* a book by Leslie Harrington and published by Benjamin Moore, is available in paint stores for $11.95, or call Benjamin Moore Paints at 1-800-826-2623.

Paint Stick—Try the Paint Stick. The handle is a hollow tube with a plunger that sucks up about a pint of paint directly from the can and delivers it to the wall through a perforated roller. It gives a more even finish and saves time. Made by HomeRight, the Paint Stick costs $29.99. Call 1-800-264-5442.

Painting—Learn to paint with oils, acrylics, or water colors. Barb's mom hadn't drawn or painted (other than household painting) since she was a child in school. In her late forties, she took an art class at a community college and has been hooked ever since. She discovered a hidden talent, and her paintings are truly beautiful (says her objective daughter!). This is one example of how someone's life can be changed through a new hobby, and she has made many new friends along the way. Some artists she knows have had their paintings printed as greeting cards.

Peace and Quiet — Peace and quiet are necessary while you're trying to think of something new. Turn off the television or radio. Just be quiet and let yourself think. Be by yourself periodically. Let your creative juices flow. If you have a lot of noise and confusion in your life, snatch a moment now and then for your project. Go for a walk without the earphones. Keep a note pad with you at all times to jot down your ideas. Pinpoint what you want to think of. Then forget about it. In the middle of the night when it's quiet and you have the time, answers will come to you. Get out of bed and write down your thoughts. Don't think to yourself, "That's a good idea. I'll remember it for morning." Unfortunately, in the morning you won't remember anything except that you had a great idea. Get up and write down the gist of your idea. Much of this book was drafted in this manner — in the middle of the night.

> *The mind is a strange machine which can combine the materials offered to it in the most astonishing ways.*
>
> **—Bertrand Russell**

Peanut Butter Cookies — This recipe for peanut butter cookies is unique in that there is no flour in it. For those who suffer from celiac disorder, recipes that don't contain flour are a real treat. (See the entry "Gluten-Free" for more information on gluten-free food.)

> 12-ounce jar of peanut butter (We think Jif has the best flavor.)
> 1 cup sugar
> 1 teaspoon vanilla
> 2 egg whites beaten stiff

Combine peanut butter, sugar, and vanilla; mix well. Fold in beaten egg whites. Roll dough into small balls and place on an ungreased cookie sheet. Use a fork to flatten each ball into a cookie form. Bake at 375 degrees for 8 minutes.

People Fifty and Older — Market something to people fifty and older, or write something for or about them. This age group controls 77 percent of all financial assets in the U.S. and 50 percent of all discretionary income. In 1996, when the oldest of the Baby Boomers turned fifty, someone was turning fifty every seven-and-a-half seconds. Do a little research and some thinking: What does this group like? What don't they like? What do they need? What will they need? In the case of the Baby Boomers and the X Generation, how did you cope or live at their ages of thirty, forty, or fifty? What special needs do they have that you could fill? Is there something that you can sell to them or do for them? Think about special needs of the elderly, handicapped, women, minorities, at-risk youth, and other unique populations.

Pets — If you don't have a pet, think about getting one. Pets can be wonderful companions that give you lots of warm, fuzzy feelings. They do need a lot of love, care, and attention, so be sure having a pet will fit in with your lifestyle. If you can't own a pet, volunteer at an animal shelter.

Pet-Sitting: It's very hard for people to leave their pets with just anybody while they're away. Pet-sitting is a service you can provide either in your home (be aware of your city's ordinances regarding animals) or at the owners' homes. Check with other pet boarding services to determine what you can charge for these services in your area. You'll have no problem getting repeat business and referrals.

Purina Pets for People: Local humane organizations give pets to people sixty years and over. Purina pays for most fees just to save homeless pets and give them to people who will enjoy them. Call 1-314-982-2261 or write to Purina Pets for People, Checkerboard Square, OCA, St. Louis, MO 63164.

Sick pets: Round-the-clock consultation is offered by the National Animal Poison Control Center at the University of

Illinois College of Veterinary Medicine. Call them at 1-800-548-2423. The cost is $30 per case. Pet first-aid help is also available at http://www.cyg.net/~rsimmons/stjohn.html .

Photo Albums — When you organize your photos in albums, add the names of places and people, and dates where applicable. If you have trouble remembering information about a snapshot, go ahead and put it in the album anyway. When you're sharing your photo albums with family and friends, somebody else may remember what you don't, and then you can add the information.

Photography — Take pictures of places you visit and people you see. Put together a photo album to keep your photos organized. Take a photography course and develop your creative photography skills. Some of your pictures could be enlarged and made into unique gifts for family and friends. Have your portrait taken, or that of the whole family.

Picnic — Enjoy a picnic in the park. You can do this with a friend, with children, or by yourself. Take a book to read or a game to play. You'll be sure to relax and enjoy yourself!

Places to Retire — Read the book *The 50 Best Retirement Communities in America* by Fred Lee (St. Martin's Press, Inc., $14.95).

Plants — Learn about edible and medicinal plants. Grow, buy, sell, and trade plants of all kinds. Offer to maintain plants in a community building or public space.

Plays—Attend plays and performances put on by your local high schools and colleges.

Poetry—Do you enjoy reading poetry or writing poetry? Keep your eyes and ears open for poetry gatherings both far and near.

Examples of Gatherings: The Colorado Cowboy Poetry Gathering occurs in January during the annual stock show in Denver, Colorado. This event was fashioned after The Gathering in Elko, Nevada, which was started more than a decade ago and is known worldwide. These gatherings offer lots of rhyme from men and women who work the land; authentic Western music; plenty of humor; and real cowboy food. There is also the World Poetry Bout Association's annual Taos Poetry Circus. During June, it is held at locations all over the city and in the Taos Pueblo. For information call 1-505-758-1800 or write to WPBA at 232 Paseo del Pueblo Sur, Taos, NM 87571.

Poetry Contests: Enter one through the National Library of Poetry, Suite 2187, One Poetry Plaza, Owings Mills, MD 21117. This contest is open to everyone and entry is free. Send in only one original poem, any subject, any style, no longer than twenty lines, with your name and address at the top of the page. You can also enter the contest online at http://www.poetry.com . The phone number is 1-410-848-4250. Call for contest dates.

If I feel physically as if the top of my head were taken off, I know that is poetry.

—Emily Dickinson

Poisons—Be careful with the following home products, which can be dangerous if swallowed or, in some cases, touched. Many cause severe damage to eyes. Some should be used only with proper ventilation, as they are dangerous to breathe. Be sure all products listed below are kept out of reach of children. Keep containers clearly labeled and properly stored. Discard expired products. The number for Poison Control is 1-800-962-1253. Post it near your telephone.

- alcohol (rubbing and liquor)
- antidepressant and heart medications
- antifreeze, brake fluids, solvents
- cleaning products
- furniture polish
- iron supplements
- lamp oil
- paint thinner and petroleum products
- perfumes
- pesticides
- tobacco products of all kinds

Police — Volunteer to work for the police department. Take a police academy course for civilians, if one is available to you. It's an interesting experience.

Privacy — Send for the free booklet *Protecting Your Privacy,* a consumer card from the Consumer Information Center, Department 583A, Pueblo, CO 81009.

PSA Test — Men should have a PSA (prostate-specific antigen) screening test done regularly. For more facts, write to The American Prostate Society, Department J375, 1340 Charwood Road, Hanover, MD 21076. Eat a diet rich in fruits and vegetables to reduce your risk of prostate cancer.

Pumpkin — Enter a pumpkin growing or a pumpkin decorating contest.

Quebec — Study the history and culture of Quebec. Plan and enjoy a trip there. Pick other cities or regions of interest to you.

Quilting — An art derived from necessity many years ago, quilting has become popular again in recent years. Quilting techniques are now used to make beautiful wall hangings and delightful articles of clothing. Classes and information are offered through fabric stores, colleges, public television stations; many areas also have quilting groups. Consult your local Yellow Pages under *Quilting* for stores that specialize in quilting, or contact Hearthside Quilts, P.O. Box 429, Shelburne, VT 05482-0429. Their phone is 1-800-451-3533.

Quire, Quoin, Quotidian — Look up words you don't recognize. Buy a Scrabble dictionary and challenge someone to an exciting game. Stimulate your brain this way.

Quit Smoking — If you're still smoking after all the public health information you've heard and read, it's time to quit. You may lengthen your life. Bones get more fragile as we age, and that is why older people are more prone to fractures. Smoking inhibits the regeneration of new bone in fractures. Try acupuncture to help you quit. Visit the Quit Smoking QuitNet at http://www.quitnet.org/ .

Races— You don't need to place a bet to enjoy being at the races. Attend greyhound races, the wiener dog nationals, frog races, horse races, car races, drag races, or motocross.

Radio Controlled— Try radio-controlled or battery-operated cars, boats, and planes. Are you interested in ham radio? Here are a couple of websites: http://home.pi.net/~dx/dutchham.html or http://www.qth.com/#ham . Also look for magazines at a local bookstore or newsstand.

Reading— How many of us love to read but have had very little time to do so? Now's your chance to catch up on those mystery, science fiction, old western, romance novels, and bestsellers you've been wishing you had time to curl up with. Go to a book signing and meet the author. Some places allow you to register to curl up in a chair in a bookstore window and read for an hour.

Real Estate— Buy, sell, trade, fix up, or rent real estate. Study for your realtor's license.

Recall a Storm— Recall a crippling blizzard, storm, or tornado in your town, and write a story about it. Submit it to the local paper.

Recipes — Put together a book or booklet of some of your family's favorite recipes, and then have copies made for family members or anyone you choose.

Reconcile — To help yourself repair relationships, read *The Solo Partner: Repairing Your Relationship on Your Own* by Phil DeLuca (Hartley & Marks, $14.95). April 2 should be Reconciliation Day, according to Ann Landers. She suggests writing a letter or making a phone call on April 2 in order to mend a broken relationship.

Recycle — It's being done everywhere. Maybe you can figure out a way to use or manufacture recycled materials. Consider installing a plastic fence made of recycled plastic milk, water, and bleach jugs. This option has saved thousands of trees from the sawmills. Contact Recycled Plastic Products at 1-800-235-7940.

Reflexology — Have your feet massaged at a reflexology clinic. Treating your feet will work wonders for your whole body.

Refurbish — Do you enjoy refurbishing things like cars, furniture, or even houses? Refurbishing can be a hobby or an idea for a small business.

*P*eace is when time doesn't matter as it passes by.

—Maria Schell

Relax — Learn to relax. This may take a while. You don't have to punch a time clock or account for every minute. The only time you need to set the alarm clock is to make an early tee time, to go motorcycling, or to play tennis. It's all right to take a leisurely stroll, have a nap after lunch, and visit with the neighbors. To help you relax, lift your eyebrows toward the ceiling; drop your jaw toward the floor. Then drop your shoulders toward the floor and move your elbows out away from your body.

Order an audiotape called *Relaxation for Busy People* by Robin Silverman and Duane Cariveau. It has three programs: the Quickie Recharge, the Night-Night Special, and a meditation to help people manage chronic or acute pain. Contact Makoche Recording at 1-800-286-9903. The cost is $11.95 plus shipping.

Remarriage—A new marriage can be wonderfully exciting, but be aware of the risks. The woman, for instance, may lose her deceased husband's pension. Check with Social Security or other pension plan provider. You may want to consider premarital agreements.

 **Rendezvous**—Attend a Mountain Man Rendezvous, which is a festival recreating the West's mountain man days. Participants dress in period costumes and reenact mountain man activities. For further information on activities, dates, and locations, contact the National Muzzle Loading Association in Friendship, Indiana, at 1-812-667-5131.

Rental Property—Clean up your rental property. In Syracuse, New York, city officials are shaming delinquent landlords into fixing up eyesore properties. They are putting up front-yard signs that read "Slum Property" and listing the owner's name, address, and phone number along with a caption saying the house violates city codes and significantly contributes to blight in the neighborhood.

Retire—Retire where it's cheaper to live, where your support system is, where your family is, or where the neighborhood caters to seniors.

If you obey all the rules, you miss all the fun.

—Katharine Hepburn

Retired Friends—You need friends who are also retired. When people are first married, they suddenly don't have as much in common with their single friends. It's like that for you now. You won't have as much in common with working friends.

Retirement Fund—Will Social Security be bankrupt by the year 2020? You will definitely need your own savings, stocks, annuities, or bonds.

One of the signs of passing youth is the birth of a sense of fellowship with other human beings as we take our place among them.

—Virginia Woolf

Romance—Enhance your romance with a Dreamscape (formerly FantaSuite) experience. You'll find suite themes from Caesar's Court and Sherwood Forest to the futuristic Space Odyssey. Robes, chocolates, flowers, and baskets are available at some locations. Following is a listing of locations and their phone numbers. Be sure to call for a picturesque brochure of the suite themes being offered. Gift certificates are also available.

Heritage Inn Greeley, Colorado	1-800-759-7829
Greenwood Inn & FantaSuite Hotel Greenwood, Indiana	1-800-444-7829
Econolodge Muscatine, Iowa	1-800-234-7829
Quality Inn & Suites Burnsville, Minnesota	1-800-666-7829
Don Q Inn Dodgeville, Wisconsin	1-800-666-7848
West Bend Inn West Bend, Wisconsin	1-800-727-9727

Roosevelt Memorial—Visit the new 7.5-acre Franklin Delano Roosevelt Memorial on the Mall in Washington, DC.

Run Errands—Provide courier service for lawyers or real estate offices. Some couriers go by bicycle or rollerblades and some by automobile. Take your pick.

Running—Run in a 5-km or 10-km race for a charity or special event or cause. Train with *The Runner's Bible* by Marc Bloom (Doubleday, $12.95).

Safety in Your Car—To deter criminals, buy a mask, stuff it with rags, fasten the mask on top of a pillow, put a man's jacket around the pillow and a man's hat on top of the mask, prop the dummy up in the front seat, and you'll have what looks like a passenger riding with you. There's safety in company.

Save Money on Greeting Cards—Write your friends a silly poem. Print it by hand or on your computer on plain or parchment paper. With the help of a rhyming dictionary and a little time, you can come up with a personalized greeting they'll love.

Save Money on Haircuts—Learn to cut your own hair and family members' hair. Do it yourself three or four times and then have a salon or barber shop cut it the next time. After a little practice, you may find your haircuts aren't so bad.

Say No! — Say no to people who want to waste your time. If you're not interested, just say no!

And then, not expecting it, you become middle-aged and anonymous. No one notices you. You achieve a wonderful freedom. It is a positive thing. You can move about, unnoticed and invisible.

—Doris Lessing

Scams — Seniors should be aware of scam strategies and ways to protect themselves from scams. Be very cautious of door-to-door and telephone solicitations. You have a right to cancel a purchase made over the phone or by door-to-door solicitation up to three days from the date of purchase. Beware of seminars or workshops that are advertised by flyers left in the mailbox or on your doorstep. Be very cautious about signing documents without getting an attorney's advice. The phone number for the National Fraud Information Center is 1-800-876-7060.

When a rogue kisses you, count your teeth.

—Hebrew Proverb

School — Go back to school! Take classes, or get another degree. Maybe you're interested in the arts, photography, the history of other countries, astronomy, crafts, or almost anything else. Goodness only knows what adventures and experiences can evolve from going back to school.

Science — Learn about scientific phenomena. If you're interested in science, find out about a program sponsored by the Museum of Science in Boston that teams children in grades four through nine with scientists who volunteer as pen-pal mentors. It's called Science-by-Mail. "Three times a year, Science-by-Mail sends student members activity packets that contain 'a big challenge' and the materials and experiments to solve the challenge. The children correspond by letter with their scientists, who offer ideas, advice and encouragement." [Source: *Denver Post*; excerpt from an article by Carol Kreck] Contact Science-by-Mail, Science Park, Boston, MA 02114-1099 or call 1-800-729-3300.

Science Books for Children — Buy the *Magic School Bus* books by Joanna Cole and Bruce Degen (Scholastic, $14.95) for your favorite children. The bus driver is a frizzy-haired teacher named Ms. Frizzle, who dresses bizarrely and takes the kids on trips to the water works, digestive tract, solar system, and ocean floor. Teachers and children love these books. Many titles are available on audiocassette.

Science Newsletter — Subscribe to the *Family Explorer* newsletter by Larry Sessions, and enjoy simple kitchen chemistry science experiments with your grandchildren or neighbors. The cost is $14.95 for a year. Write to Family Explorer, 6874 East Harvard Avenue, Denver, CO 80225.

The voice of the sea speaks to the soul. The touch of the sea is sensuous, enfolding the body in its soft, close embrace.

—Kate Chopin

Sea — Are you drawn to life on the sea, or in the sea? Do you enjoy sailing, deep sea fishing, snorkeling, or scuba diving? Do you want to live by the sea? Would you be interested in underwater photography? Coral or abalone harvesting? Hunting for sunken treasure or ships?

Seasonal Contests—Start seasonal contests for guessing when the first measurable snowfall will occur; when the first robin or crocus will appear; when ice-out will happen at Moosehead Lake, Maine; and so on.

Sell—If you're interested in network marketing, sell Amway, Avon, Fuller Brush, Nu-Skin, Shaklee, Stanley Home Products, Tupperware, or products for another company. If you want to sell your home, buy the book *How to Sell Your Own Home* by William Supple, Jr. (Picket Fence Publishing, $14.95). Call 1-800-761-6060 to order. Visit the national network of For Sale By Owner websites at http//www.nfsboa.com .

Senior Centers—They're full of activities with arts and crafts, bridge, dancing, day trips and excursions, and health and exercise equipment.

> *You need someone to love you while you're looking for someone to love.*
>
> **—Shelagh Delaney**

Senior Discounts and Bargains—Ask for senior discounts. You won't get them if you don't ask. Airline tickets and hotel rooms may be discounted (see also Appendix F). Restaurants often offer senior discounts, and so do retail stores such as Montgomery Ward, Sears, auto stores, and golf shops. Contact a large local bank for possible senior travel clubs. Many have them. Just ask. Request furniture discounts and catalogs by calling Cherry Hill Furniture at 1-800-328-0933 and National Decorators at 1-800-955-2559. For drugs by mail, two companies that have very favorable pricing are Diversified Prescription at 1-800-452-1976 and Medi-Mail at 1-800-922-3444.

Senior Resorts—Plan to vacation at retirement community destinations where mature travelers can obtain inexpensive rental units that make resort vacationing affordable. Usually only one person in the couple must be fifty-five or older; you have to spend some time touring the property and listening to a sales pitch. [The following three examples are reprinted with permission of *The Orange County Register*, copyright 1994.]

Northwest Arkansas: Here you will find a gentle climate, a low cost of living, and good housing. Arkansas is second only to Florida in its percentage of retirees. Newcomers are lured by parklike retirement communities for people with active lifestyles. According to one brochure, Bella Vista Village is the largest retirement community in the Ozarks. More than 6,000 homes are tucked into this rolling 36,000 acre preserve about thirty miles north of Fayetteville near the Missouri border. There are seven golf courses and seven lakes. At Bella Vista Village, visitors get guest cards for low-cost golf. Contact Bella Vista Village, Community Relations Department, 432 Town Center, Bella Vista, AR 72714 (1-800-553-6687).

Sun Cities in the Southwest: You can stay in furnished homes in Palm Springs (1-800-533-5932); in Tucson (1-800-422-8483); near Phoenix (1-800-528-2604); and near Las Vegas (1-800-987-9875).

Tampa Bay, Florida: You can spend up to a week in Sun City Center, a retirement community twenty miles south of Tampa that is home to about 13,000 senior citizens. Contact Sun City Center, P.O. Box 5698, Sun City Center, FL 33571-5698 or call 1-800-237-8200.

Sewing— Do you enjoy sewing? Do you know how to sew? There are many different types of sewing to fill in a few of those retirement hours/days. Maybe you enjoy making alterations (which can be a small business for you), making window treatments, working with upholstery, sewing crafts, designing clothes, or making patterns. Maybe you have an idea that involves sewing and would fill a special niche—for example, you might create clothing for people with special medical needs or disabilities. Barb read of a woman who created custom-fitted bedding sheets for boat owners, and another woman who designed clothes that were works of art. The possibilities are as extensive as your imagination. Another idea is to sew all night at one of the enterprising sewing machine companies that host all-night sewing marathons every year. You bring in your machine and whatever you want to work on, and share munchies with other people there.

Sex—Sex may be more enjoyable, leisurely, and creative with more time available. The many pleasures of sex, with and without intercourse, are described in the book *Ask Me Anything: A Sex Therapist Answers the Most Important Questions for the '90s* by Marty Klein (Pacifica Press, $16.95).

> T*he mind can also be an erogenous zone.*
>
> **—Raquel Welch**

Share—Share any special talent, skill, folklore, or knowledge. Form a group and teach your specialty to others. Share your magazines and investment and medical newsletters with others.

Shopping—Do you absolutely love to shop? Would you be interested in running a service business of shopping for people who are too busy or unable to shop? You could do their grocery shopping, or their shopping for gifts, household items, et cetera. You work within their budget, use their money, and charge them a fee for your time (and imagination).

> W*e look into mirrors but we only see the effects of our times on us—not our effects on others.*
>
> **—Pearl Bailey**

Sign Language— Learn American Sign Language or teach it to others.

Silence— Go somewhere to enjoy silence for a weekend. Try a convent, an abbey, an ashram, or a retreat. There are 1200 listings in *Sanctuaries* by Marcia Kelly (Random House, $15.00).

My personal hobbies are reading, listening to music, and silence.

—Edith Sitwell

Sing-a-Longs— They're fun at the piano or organ. Have copies of the words handy and invite a good piano player.

Sister Cities Program— This program pairs towns in the United States with towns in foreign countries. The arrangement provides opportunities for educational, cultural, and technical interchanges. Students and teachers visit their sister city schools, fire and police departments, and town offices and then exchange ideas. Citizens can often arrange vacation visits or house swaps. The program has a waiting list of cities wanting to pair up. For more information, contact the Sister Cities Program at 120 South Payne Street, Alexandria, VA 22314 or call 1-703-836-3535.

 Skiing— You'll have more time to enjoy snow- or water-skiing. If you don't ski already, it's never too late to take lessons! After your seventieth birthday, you may ski free at Winter Park, Colorado.

 Sleep— Get a better night's sleep. You may want to try an air bed made by Innomax. Call 1-303-298-0230. Cuddle Ewe sells an all-wool mattress cover that can be fluffed up, turned over, and taken out and aired. Contact D. L. Anderson and Associates, Inc., 10650 County Road 81, Suite U, Maple Grove, MN 55369 or call 1-800-328-9493. The National Sleep Foundation offers a free pamphlet called *When You Can't Sleep: ABC's of ZZZ's.* Write to 729 Fifteenth Street, NW, 4th Floor, Washington, DC 20005. Include a 55-cent stamped, self-addressed, business-sized envelope.

Sleigh Ride — Take a sleigh ride in a winter wonderland, or a hay ride any time of year. What a romantic idea!

Slow Food Movement — Join an international group out of Italy specializing in leisurely eating. Subscription to their journal is $44 (U.S.). Write to Slow Food Movement, Servizio Abbonamenti, Via Mendicita Istruita 45, 12042 BRA (CN) Italy. Their website address is http://www.slow-food.com .

> For fast-acting relief, try slowing down.
>
> —Lily Tomlin

Smile — If you meet someone without a smile, give him one of yours.

Spend — Spend some money on yourself. You deserve it!

Spirituality — Your spiritual side may be of special interest at this stage in your life. Attend your place of worship. Make peace with your God. Attend or teach religious education classes. Participate in social groups at your place of worship.

Sports — Take up one of these popular participatory sports: swimming, exercise walking, or bike riding. The most popular spectator sports are horse racing, professional baseball, and college basketball.

. . . .

Sports Vision Training—Check out sports vision training to help your golf, tennis, baseball, or volleyball game. For the name of a specialist in your town, call the American Optometric Association's sports vision section at 1-314-991-4100.

Start Your Own Business—This can provide you with some "mad" money, or you can launch a whole new career. You decide! Are you an entrepreneur? Have you ever dreamed of owning your own business? You're never too old. An entrepreneur's most important qualifications are strong organizational skills, good business sense, some financial sophistication, and a willingness to work hard. You can start your own business, buy an existing business, or buy a franchise and receive guidance from those who know what it takes to make a business successful. The book you are reading right now contains some business ideas, and Appendix D provides some information on starting your own business. Most libraries offer literature full of advice on starting a business, choosing a business to start, bookkeeping for your business, obtaining legal advice, and so on.

Luck is a matter of preparation meeting opportunity.

—Oprah Winfrey

Community colleges almost always offer classes to help you with your small business. You may also want to read *Starting a Mini-Business: A Guidebook for Seniors* by Nancy Olsen (Fair Oaks Publishing, $8.95); *Homemade Money: How to Select, Start, Manage, Market and Multiply the Profits of a Business at Home* by Barbara Brabec (F&W Publications, $19.99); and *Blueprint for Success: The Complete Guide to Starting a Business after 50* by Albert Myers (Newcastle, $12.95).

State Parks—State parks welcome volunteers. Consider helping out with tours, trail maintenance, story telling, or in the gift shop. Enjoy the beautiful scenery and working with the public!

Statue Repair and Cleaning — Do you know how to clean and repair crumbling concrete statues? Do a beautifying project around your town.

Stick Ball — Teach kids the game of stickball using a broom handle and a rubber ball. No uniforms or special training are needed. A group called the Guardian Angels is teaching this game around the country.

Stock Review — Stocks, bonds, mutual funds, and investments of all kinds need periodic review. Make an appointment with your financial advisor to do this if you are an investor.

Storybooks — Make cassette recordings of yourself animatedly reading favorite children's stories. Send the books and tapes to grandchildren, nieces, and nephews. Maybe they will request subsequent titles.

 Stress — Control stress. Read the book *Nature's Prozac* by Judith Sachs (Prentice-Hall, $22.95).

Study Cartooning — Contact a community college, library, art institute, or bookstore to inquire about classes in cartooning.

Sunday Brunch — Go out to Sunday brunch. Consider taking your extended family to brunch once a year.

Sweepstakes Scams — If you're the victim of a sweepstakes scam, contact the Postal Inspection Service, 475 L'Enfant Plaza West, SW, Washington, DC 20260, which tips off the post office in cases involving U.S. Mail services. Also notify your state attorney general's office, FTC (Federal Trade Commission), FBI (Federal Bureau of Investigation), and BBB (Better Business Bureau). To check the legitimacy of a sweepstakes before entering, contact the BBB or state attorney general's office.

T

Tai Chi — Learn tai chi, a uniquely relaxing, invigorating dancelike exercise. Gentle physical movements help to connect and lubricate the joints while cultivating chi energy throughout the body. Check your bookstore, library, or continuing education program for information on tai chi. Martial arts studios often offer tai chi classes.

Taxes — Consult an expert to help you save money on taxes or to set up trusts to protect your money.

Teach — You probably have valuable knowledge and experiences that can be passed on to others, whatever your area of expertise: religion, education, business, athletics, or other area. If teaching appeals to you, particularly as part-time work, check with community colleges, your place of worship, and community groups of interest to you. Maybe you have a hobby you've enjoyed for years and would like to share with others. Teach kids in scout groups and other organizations some of the games you played as a child. You'll get back as much as you give.

> **G**ive a man a fish, and you feed him for a day. Teach a man to fish, and you feed him for a lifetime.
>
> **—Chinese Proverb**

Teachers International — Teach in a foreign country for two or more years. Contact International School Services, 15 Roszel Road, P.O. Box 5910, Princeton, NJ 08543 (phone 1-609-452-0990; fax 1-609-452-2690; e-mail iss@iss.edu; website http://www.iss.edu). They establish and operate schools, place teachers and administrators, and purchase and ship curricular materials and school supplies. They also publish a bimonthly newsletter titled *NewsLinks*. Another organization of this type is the Overseas Placement Service for Educators, University of Northern Iowa, Cedar Falls, IA, 50614.

 Teeth — If you have dentures, wear them for three reasons: (1) Not wearing dentures can cause the gums to change and then the dentures won't fit properly; (2) the face looks much better with teeth; and (3) gradual hearing loss can result from not wearing your dentures. If you are not wearing your dentures because they fit improperly, find a dentist who will work to get a proper fit. Brighten your smile with the Rembrandt Dazzling White At-Home bleaching system and toothpaste in one, which you can find at the supermarket (or call 1-800-548-3663). It will bleach your teeth up to five shades whiter. A million-dollar smile is hard to beat. See your dentist for a professional consultation. Laser tooth whitening is a brand new innovation to ask about also.

Tetanus Shot — Get a tetanus booster shot. Tetanus can result from even a minor wound or scratch. Seventy percent of tetanus infections occur in people over the age of fifty, and this age group is the least likely to be immunized.

Theater — Attend a melodrama. Go to plays. Join a theater group and act; be an understudy; work on set decorations or costumes; be a gofer or a promoter.

Theme Cruises — These are popular because they provide passengers with both an ideal vacation and the opportunity to indulge in a special interest. Try a cruise themed on jazz, gardening, world affairs, sports, fitness, nutrition, big band music, bridge, country music, murder mystery, photography, or routes of the great explorers. For further information on itineraries, travel dates, and prices, contact a travel agent, or call the cruise line directly (see Appendix F).

T*he cure for anything is salt water—sweat, tears, or the sea.*

—Isak Dinesen

Theme Parties — Throw a wonderful theme party complete with set decorations. Themes could include Caribbean Cruise, Phantom of the Opera, Casino, and many other possibilities. In the Denver area, you would contact Greg or Chris Reinke at 1-303-781-2001. At Halloween they host the Haunted Mansion at 4211 South Natches Court (at Santa Fe and Oxford) in Denver. They also have thousands of costumes (including sumo wrestling costumes), masks, gifts, makeup, and accessories for sale or rent. If a similar business doesn't exist in your area, that needn't stop you from devising the party yourself or with others.

This Is Your Life — Make a "This Is Your Life" video for yourself or for the birthday or anniversary of someone you love. Equipment you will need includes one TV, one video camera, two VCRs (VCR #1 is to record from, and VCR #2 has a blank tape on which to record to), one editor, and one video enhancer/stereo/audio mixer. This equipment is available at electronics/stereo companies such as Soundtrack and Radio Shack. Cables to connect this to your TV should have gold-plated connectors (optional for enhanced quality). Following are step-by-step instructions on how to create this video.

1. Use double-faced tape to place photographs in chronological order on a black background against a wall. Using a video camera, videotape the photos at 4–5 seconds on each picture. Adjust with the "zoom" as needed, fade to black for endings, or blur. (*Alternative:* Instead of using photographs, you can use bits from other videos. Watch the video and take notes of the key spots you want to record. As the video tape you are taping from plays on VCR #1, hit *record* and *pause* on your editor.) Using either one of these methods gives you Tape A in VCR #2.

2. Run Tape A (your new tape) in VCR #1 and using the stereo/audio mixer you have four tracks to—
    a. add music by playing a favorite song, record, or tape or having someone play live music.
    b. add your own narration to the picture.
    c. leave the original sound from the original tape.
    d. adjust the overall sound on the resulting tape.

3. If you want to get really deluxe, you can buy a character generator and put words on the screen, or you can use handlettered or computer-generated titles.

This setup makes a delightful photo album for someone very special to you. If you plan to sell your video, use live original music so as not to get in trouble with copyright infringement. If your results are applauded by those who view your tape, this could become a business idea for you. (See Appendix D: Starting a Business.)

Tour—Go on tours. Tour a beer brewery, a tea company, a glass factory, a model railroad layout, and so on.

Toys—The Eastern Star organization of the Masonic Temple in Denver is giving stuffed toys to children involved in a police situation, traffic accident, domestic dispute, or other emergency. They call them "Toys of Love" and know that these gifts ease the child's pain. They have committed to this program for five years. Start a program like this where you live.

Trade—Trade work with other people. "You paint my house, and I'll lay your tile," or any other trade you both like the sound of.

Trains—Enjoy a trip on a train. Call Amtrak at 1-800-872-7245, or visit their website at http://www.amtrak.com . Join a model railroaders group. Build layouts from kits. Visit train museums.

Travel—Appendix F, Travel Tips, is full of travel tidbits, ideas, and information. To improve your equilibrium and balance while riding in a car, bus, or plane, refer to *Brain Gym* Activities, Appendix C.

Travel Agent—Become a travel agent or tour guide. Check the Yellow Pages of a large city under *Travel and Tourism Development and Education*.

Trekkie—If you're a Star Trek fan, go to conventions displaying memorabilia. Meet and correspond with other "Trekkies." For convention dates and locations and a chat room, visit the website http://www.wwcd.com/shows/strekconv.html . Also take a look at http://www.stwww.com and http://www.startrek.msn.com .

Typing—Are you a retired secretary or word processor? Do you really love to type? Would you like to work out of your home? College students are always looking for someone to type their papers; job hunters need résumés created or updated; small offices sometimes have overflow work for freelancers. If you are a good typist, you can take in as much work as you like. It would be very helpful to have a computer and a letter quality printer. To improve your keyboard ability, refer to *Brain Gym* Activities, Appendix C.

Unclutter—Clear out your life of things you don't need or use. Go through the house, the garage, and the attic and basement, too. Then have a garage sale and use the money you collect to do or buy something special for yourself. Alternatively, donate your goods or proceeds to a worthy cause.

Vacation Spot—Stay at the charming Seth Peterson Cottage at Lake Delton, Wisconsin, for approximately $225 per night. It was designed by Frank Lloyd Wright and is one of his smallest and final creations. Contact the Sand County Service Co. at P.O. Box 409, Lake Delton, WI 53940 or call 1-608-254-6551.

Vatican Holy Year 2000 — Make plans to stay in a remodeled convent or seminary during the Holy Year in 2000. Check with your travel agent or Rev. Vincenzo Migliaccio, Steward of the Pauline Monastery, Via Roselli, Rome. There are 141 convents, seminaries, and nunneries scheduled by the Vatican for transformation into what pundits have dubbed "holy hotels."

Veterans' Death and Burial Benefits — For veterans and their spouses, Uncle Sam provides free burial, marker, and flag in veterans' or state cemeteries. Call the Veterans Administration at 1-800-827-1000. Get *American Guidance for Seniors and Their Caregivers* by Ken Skala (Key Communication, $19.95).

Video — Make your own "how-to" video of your specialty. Find a television station that plays this kind of video. Or, make video tapes of parents, grandparents, and older relatives. Have them talk, move around, and tell a little about themselves. When these older people have died, the grandchildren and generations to come will enjoy knowing their ancestors, hearing their stories, and seeing their facial features and expressions. Several of the little ones in Tricia's family have asked, "What was grandpa or grandma like?" A video

would really help. Prepare a script for discussion while you're taping. "What was life like when you were young? How did you and so-and-so meet? What was good, bad, sad about your life? What funny things happened? Tell about food, work, and historical events going on during your life." Once you've gone to the trouble of preparing this script, you can go right into business doing videos for other families and friends.

Visit — Go see the scenic and historic spots in your state. Appreciate the natural beauty, the museums, the historic towns, the antique shops, et cetera. Take pictures of where you have been and put these together in a photo album. One benefit of being retired is that you can go to these places during the week while everyone else is working, unless you prefer to be with crowds when you sightsee. The choice is yours! Most visitor spots offer discounted admission for seniors. Some are open free one day a week. Call ahead to ask.

Volunteer — Hospitals, charitable organizations, schools, civic groups, places of worship, animal welfare societies, and social service organizations are all in need of people to volunteer their time and talents. Volunteering doesn't have to be all-consuming, since you can work as much or little as you like. Whatever you do, the rewards will be many. The Peace Corps loves retirees and has many volunteers older than sixty-five. For other ideas, refer to Appendix E, Volunteering. In your local Yellow Pages, look under *Social Service Organizations* or *Women's Organizations*.

I expect to pass through this world but once. Any good, therefore, that I can do, or any kindness that I can show to any fellow creature, let me do it now. Let me not defer or neglect it, for I shall not pass this way again.

—Stephen Grelles

Wallpaper — Put up wallpaper or a border in your living room, or in a room that is special to you. Try stenciling for an inexpensive alternative to wallpaper.

Weather Lore—This is an interesting area to study. Find out what significance folks see in the early migration of birds, an abundance of hummingbirds, the locusts' six-weeks-until-winter warning, the early ripening of chokecherries and raspberries, the rings on a woolly caterpillar, and so on. Talk to folks about weather lore, or read up on it at the library. Write an article or talk to a group about the weather lore you discover.

Weddings—Become a wedding consultant. Help make that "special day" come together for your clients. If you absolutely love to plan weddings, this could be a very rewarding career. The more you know about etiquette, religious protocols, and local retailers and services, the easier your job will be.

You can't help getting older, but you do not have to get old.

—George Burns

"Weekend" Section of Newspaper—This section publicizes all kinds of things to do. It lists comedy-drama theater, musicals, dinner theaters, and a plethora of events from antique shows to Uptown Sampler, a tour of different restaurants. There are also listings for dancing, including ballroom, senior, single, old-time, no-partner-needed, folk, round, country, hula, disco, Irish, Israeli folk, moving meditation, barn, polka, and swing. Some events are nonalcoholic and nonsmoking. The weekend section also lists auditions; nightclubs categorized by jazz, rock, country, crossover, and comedy; art shows and art galleries; nature sites and events; kids' stuff; and museum events.

Where Can I Find? Columns—Read the "Wanted" sections of local publications to see what people want to buy. You might want to begin producing or collecting and selling items in high demand.

White Water Rafting—Is it in your future?

Widows/Widowers—Join a group for widows or widowers, called WOWs, or join Parents Without Partners. Join a singles club or go to singles dances.

Helping Them Cope: When a husband or wife dies is a very trying time. Friends usually send a sympathy card or flowers, attend the funeral or memorial service, and take food for the luncheon. Afterward, there are many things you can do. Offer to help the widow/widower send out the acknowledgment cards. The person is usually very grateful for that assistance, since it makes a grim job bearable. Tricia and her husband, Bill, offer to sort through and dispose of the deceased person's belongings. Give the widow/widower some time—it may take weeks or months—but when they're ready, go through everything from jewelry to junk, tools to treasures. Have a garage sale. Help dispose of collectibles, if that is your field of expertise. Otherwise, find a knowledgable, trustworthy person to do it. Dispose of unwanted vehicles. Help the widow/widower buy a new(er) car to begin their new life. In the ensuing months, call them often. Encourage them to find new activities—golf, bridge, dancing, hobbies, travel—or possibly to move to a more suitable residence. Introduce them to others whose company they may enjoy. In time you may be welcoming their new boy/girlfriend. A friend of ours was seventy when his wife died. He said, "I figure I've only got ten more years, so I'm not going to waste a minute of it."

Wildlife—Work with wildlife in some way. Contact the Fish & Wildlife Service, the Interior Department, or the National Park Service, all listed in the phone book under United States Government.

Wills and Living Wills—These are important. Do you have them? Statistics show that 70 percent of Americans do *not*. The laws vary from state to state with regard to wills and living wills. If you have a living will, carry a copy with you. A living will won't do you any good sitting in your safe deposit box while you're lying in another state. The entry "Legal Services Made Affordable" gives information on how Pre-Paid Legal Services, Inc., can help you prepare your will.

Women Golfers — Subscribe to *Golf for Women* by calling 1-800-374-7941. The subscription price is $18.97 per year plus $2.00 postage and handling. In Canada, add $6.00. Magazine-sales services sometimes offer discounted subscriptions. Every issue offers interesting and helpful articles about your game and places to play. You'll also find ads for custom-tailored clubs, instruction, and just about anything else a woman golfer could want.

Women Keep Active — Studies show that women who exercise after menopause live longer than sedentary women. Bowling, gardening, or walking four or more times a week increased the women's lifespan by 33 percent. Moderate activity just once weekly increased women's lifespan by 12 percent. [Source: *Journal of the American Medical Association,* 4/23/97; "Active older women live longer," by Brenda C. Coleman].

Golf is a game whose aim is to hit a very small ball into an even smaller hole, with weapons singularly ill-designed for the purpose.

—Winston Churchill

Woodworking — Maybe you dream of building the projects you see in *Woodworking Magazine,* in your local newspaper, or on the PBS stations. Go for it.

Work — Do you want to work with babies, children, teens, adults, or old people? Do you work better with sick people or well people? Good kids or troubled kids? At-risk kids? Criminals or gangs? Find ways to help others by offering your services as a baby-sitter, an advocate, a hotline operator, or a caregiver. Look for ads and fliers requesting help; these often appear on public bulletin boards, at bus stops, and in newspapers. Local television stations may air agency requests for volunteers. Some organizations and individuals will pay for your time and services.

Wrinkle-Free Botox — Do away with your wrinkles, if you want to. See a dermatologist or plastic surgeon for injections of Botox (actually, the same toxin that causes botulism). A full-forehead Botox treatment costs about $500 and can make you look younger, calmer, happier, and

friendlier. The Botox treatment is only good for four months and needs to be repeated. Plastic surgery is more permanent. Ask your doctor about risks and side effects. Also investigate other types of face-lift or cosmetic surgery.

Write —

Autobiography: Write an autobiography or put together a family history. Each of us has our own "story," if we would just take the time to put it in writing. Children and grandchildren particularly enjoy hearing about their ancestors' early years. Once Grandma and Grandpa were young and in love, too, and just starting their lives together. Once they were children who played and argued. Future generations can enjoy and learn from your memories and experiences, if you record them. Adult and continuing education programs offer courses that can help you write and publish your personal and family histories.

> To grow is to change, and to have changed often is to have grown much.
>
> —John Henry Newman

Book: Do something crazy, scary, wild, and wonderful, and then write a book about it. Mike McIntyre hitchhiked from Cape Fear, North Carolina, to the Golden Gate Bridge. He went without money and accepted only rides, food, and a place to rest his head. His heartwarming story became *The Kindness of Strangers* (Berkley Publishing, $12.00). Other delightful books about trips across America include John Steinbeck's *Travels with Charley* and Peter Jenkins's *Walk Across America* and *Walk Across America 2.* These are available at your library.

Commercials, Slogans, Jingles: Send them to the appropriate businesses.

Essays: Write essays about anything and everything, the way Charles Osgood of "The Osgood Files" does. Sell them to a radio syndicate for broadcast on the radio or to a newspaper syndicate for publication.

Mystery Stories for Kids: Could you be the next R. L. Stine? He is the bestselling author of two sets of books, the *Goosebumps* series and the *Fear Street* series, both written for kids ages eight to twelve. His books are not violent; they're kind of "scary fantasies." Stine wants his tombstone to note, "He got boys to read." Once the kids are reading, a lot of librarians and parents will hope they move on to more "literary" works. Ask a librarian or bookseller for recommendations. Read a few of the books by Stine and other authors and decide which type of writing you want to emulate.

Play: Are you tired of seeing *Auntie Mame, Oklahoma,* and *Nunsense* for the umpteenth time? To improve your creative writing ability, refer to *Brain Gym* Activities, Appendix C.

Writer on Vacation — Look for stories everywhere you go. Phyllis Karas wrote fiction for teenagers before she went on vacation to Greece.

> **W**riting is the only thing that, when I do it, I do not feel I should be doing something else.
>
> —Gloria Steinem

While there, she met a woman who had been a private secretary to Aristotle and Jackie Onassis. They made a deal that fetched them a million-dollar advance for their collaborative book, tentatively titled *Jackie & Ari: The Greek Years* (Putnam; price not yet available).

Xerox—Make xerographic copies of letters and exchange them with members of your family and friends in round-robin fashion.

Year 2000 Party—Plan a memorable party for New Year's Eve 1999. What sounds fun? A cruise ship straddling the International Dateline? A supersonic jet liner pursuing the clock change across several time zones? Make your plans now—reservations are filling up!

Year 2000 Problem—Figure out a way to solve the "Year 2000 problem," which threatens to cause everything from computers and telephones to air traffic control systems to go on the fritz at the stroke of midnight, 31 December 1999. Visit the websites http://www.year2000.com and http://www.y2k-info.com . Maybe you can't solve the problem all by yourself, but if you learn enough, you can help others stay out of harm's way with regard to this "time bomb."

Yoga—Learn yoga and meditation for relaxation.

You've Tried a Dozen Things—Keep trying, even if you've tried a dozen ways to make extra money and not one has panned out. Perhaps you've been poo-pooed for everything you've tried or even talked about. Don't give up. As a friend of ours always said, "If you throw enough things against the wall, one's bound to stick sooner or later." Keep trying.

Yo-yo—Teach youngsters how to do tricks with a yo-yo.

Zip—Zip through the house periodically, cleaning and tidying up.

I hate housework! You make the beds, you do the dishes—and six months later you have to start all over again."
—Joan Rivers

Zippedy—Sing "Zippedy-Do-Dah," "Mairzy Doats," "Supercalifragilisticexpialidosious," "Abba Dabba Honeymoon," and other silly songs. Better yet, teach them to your grandchildren. Best of all, dance while you're singing.

Zoo—Zoos are great places for the young and old. Many zoos have free days for seniors weekly or several times a year. See if your local zoo needs help with tours, especially during the school year when field trips to the zoo are popular.

Zucchini Bread—What do you do with all that zucchini in your garden? Grate some and freeze it, putting two cups of grated zucchini into each freezer bag. Then pull out a bag of the premeasured zucchini any time during the year, and make yourself two loaves of zucchini bread! The recipe follows:

> Beat together well:
>> 3 eggs
>> 2 cups sugar
>> 1 cup oil
>
> Add:
>> 1 teaspoon vanilla
>> 3 cups flour
>> 1 teaspoon each of cinnamon,
>>> salt, and baking powder
>> 1/4 teaspoon baking soda
>> 2 cups grated zucchini
>> 1 cup crushed nuts or crushed drained pineapple

Pour batter into two greased and floured bread pans and bake at 350 degrees for one hour, or until knife comes out clean. If you make the bread with the pineapple, add an extra touch of flour. Barb sometimes adds grated coconut and granola cereal in place of the nuts and pineapple.

LET YOUR IMAGINATION SOAR

ACTIVITIES FROM

A TO Z

Partake of a smorgasbord of exciting ideas and activities! The following list gives cryptic explanations designed to pique your interest and whet your appetite for further study or action. Subjects run the gamut from *abacus* to *zymurgy*. Look for ideas that interest you, even remotely, and mark them for consideration now or sometime in the future. (If this is a library book, splurge and get your own copy to mark, or use a notebook.)

Topic	Interested?			Remarks
	Yes	No	Later	
ABACUS Learn to use one.				
ABALONE Buy jewelry made of abalone shell; fish for/eat abalone.				
ABROAD Travel to foreign countries.				
ABSTRACT Study/create abstract art.				
ABUSE Help abused men/women/children.				
ACCORDION Learn to play the accordion.				
ACROBATICS Teach/coach acrobatics.				
ACTIVE Stay active/alert/sociable.				

Topic	Interested?			Remarks
	Yes	No	Later	
ACUPUNCTURE Study/try as treatment for pain.				
ADDICT Work with drug addicts.				
AEROBICS Exercise your lungs and heart.				
AFGHAN Knit/crochet an afghan for your naps.				
AFRICA Study African history/culture/ issues.				
AIRPLANE Collect/build/fly model airplanes.				
ALCOHOLISM Don't drink much; help someone who drinks too much.				
ALLIGATOR Go alligator hunting.				
AMARYLLIS Give someone this lovely plant.				
AMERICA Study/teach American history or geography.				

Topic	Interested?			Remarks
	Yes	No	Later	
AMPUTEE Help someone less fortunate.				
AMUSE Learn to amuse yourself and/or others.				
ANIMAL Offer to walk people's dogs; baby-sit people's hamsters/ birds/fish.				
ANTARCTIC Study the region south of the Antarctic Circle.				
ANTARES Study the giant red star in the constellation Scorpio.				
APHID Learn about gardening/ insects/diseases.				
ARTIST Learn to create pictures/ sculptures.				
AUCTION Buy/sell items at auction, or just attend one.				
AUDIENCE Be a part of the audience of your favorite talk show.				

Topic	Interested?			Remarks
	Yes	No	Later	
AUSTRALIA Visit Australia; study penal colony history.				
AVATAR Study Hindu mythology.				
BABEL Study this Biblical city.				
BABY-SIT Sit grandchildren/neighbors' children occasionally.				
BAGUETTE Study/buy/sell gems; make jewelry.				
BAIZE Restore pool table; cover with this fabric.				
BAKE Learn to cook/bake.				
BALKAN PENINSULA Study/visit Greece or Turkey.				
BAND Form a group of musicians; entertain.				
BANJO Learn to play the banjo.				

Topic	Interested?			Remarks
	Yes	No	Later	
BARBECUE Have a barbecue; invite friends.				
BARBELL Exercise/weight train.				
BARBERSHOP Join a quartet; entertain others.				
BARTENDER Work as a bartender.				
BASEBALL Play/coach/attend baseball games.				
BASILICA Study/visit famous cathedrals/ basilicas.				
BATTERY Replace the battery in your car.				
BEACHCOMBER Walk/vacation on the beach.				
BEDRIDDEN Visit/read to/cheer up bedridden people.				
BESTSELLER Read; join a book club; discuss books.				
BICYCLE Ride for fun and exercise.				

Topic	Interested?			Remarks
	Yes	No	Later	
BLINTZ Make thin pancakes folded over cheese or fruit.				
BLOOD BANK Volunteer/give blood.				
BODY LANGUAGE Perceive attitudes that are communicated through body language.				
BOOMERANG Buy curved missile that returns to thrower.				
BORSCHT Make beet soup hot or cold.				
BOW Practice shooting arrows.				
BOXER Study Chinese secret society action of 1900.				
BOXING Watch/teach/coach boxing.				
BRAILLE Study/teach braille.				
BRAINSTORM Share ideas/inspiration with others.				

Topic	Interested?			Remarks
	Yes	No	Later	
BRASS BAND Listen to/join a brass band.				
BRONTOSAURUS Study dinosaurs of the Jurassic period.				
BUDDHISM Study the doctrines of this Eastern religion.				
BULL MARKET Follow the stock market.				
BYZANTIUM Learn about the ancient city on the site of Istanbul.				
CABINETMAKER Make/buy fine wood furniture.				
CACTUS Visit a desert in springtime.				
CALLIGRAPHY Study/practice beautiful penmanship.				
CAMARADERIE Enjoy friendly good will among comrades.				
CAMPAIGN Work for/against political candidates.				

Topic	Interested?			Remarks
	Yes	No	Later	
CARTOON Learn how to draw cartoons.				
CASINO Have fun gambling (if you can control it!).				
CATALOG Order merchandise from a catalog.				
CAUCUS Attend a political caucus.				
CENTERPIECE Create a gorgeous centerpiece for your table.				
CERAMICS Learn to make ceramics/ pottery/porcelain.				
CHEMOTHERAPY Help/visit someone taking chemotherapy.				
CHESS Play chess; enter tournaments.				
CHILI CON CARNE Enter a chili-making or chili-eating contest.				
CHIPPENDALE Study/buy rococo/18th-century furniture.				

Topic	Interested?			Remarks
	Yes	No	Later	
CHRISTIANITY Study the history of Christianity.				
CIRCUS Attend a circus/pageant/fair.				
CIVIL WAR Study the Civil War.				
CLAY PIGEON Try trapshooting.				
CLEF Learn to read/play music.				
CLIMATOLOGY Study the science of climates.				
CLUTCH Fix/repair your car.				
COAT OF ARMS Study your family coat of arms/heraldry.				
COLOSSEUM Visit the Roman amphitheater.				
COMIC BOOK Collect/buy/sell/trade comic books.				
COMMON MARKET Study the European Economic Community.				

Topic	Interested?			Remarks
	Yes	No	Later	
COMPLEMENT Find a friend and provide for each other's needs.				
CONGRESS Write/call your senator/ representative.				
CONSOLE Comfort someone in sorrow.				
CONTESTANT Be a contestant on your favorite TV game show.				
CONTINENTAL CONGRESS Study legislative bodies of 1774–1781.				
COPPERHEAD Study North American snakes.				
COPYRIGHT Write something and obtain a copyright.				
COUNTRY DANCE Learn to country/line/square dance.				
COUSIN Get together with your cousin(s).				
COVERED WAGON Study the American pioneers.				

Topic	Interested?			Remarks
	Yes	No	Later	
CPR Take a course to get/renew your cardiopulmonary resuscitation certificate.				
CRANIOLOGY Study the structure/characteristics of skulls.				
CREATIVE Create something new/new ways to do things.				
CREWEL Learn this form of embroidery.				
CRICKET Play cricket with bat, ball, and wickets.				
CRIMINOLOGY Study crime/criminals; visit prisoners.				
CRO-MAGNON Study prehistoric human found in France.				
CROQUET Play croquet with wooden mallets and balls.				
CROSS-COUNTRY SKI Go cross-country skiing.				

Topic	Interested?			Remarks
	Yes	No	Later	
CRUISE Take a nice cruise.				
CUBA Study Cuba's history/politics/problems.				
CURLING IRON Use a curling iron on your hair.				
DAGUERREOTYPE Study early photographic process.				
DAR Join Daughters of the American Revolution.				
DARTS Throw darts at a bull's-eye; join a dart league.				
DEBRIS Remove debris from a garden/vacant lot/river.				
DECLARATION OF INDEPENDENCE Read it again.				
DELFT Collect blue-and-white tableware.				

Topic	Interested?			Remarks
	Yes	No	Later	
DENDROLOGY Study trees.				
DESIGN Design your new house/ clothing/decor.				
DIABETES Be checked for diabetes.				
DIAMOND Sell/collect diamonds/jewelry.				
DILL PICKLE Make a crock of dill pickles.				
DIORAMA Build a miniature scene with figures and background.				
DIRIGIBLE Study lighter-than-air aircraft.				
DO IT YOURSELF Build something in the house.				
DOLL Collect/buy/sell/refurbish dolls.				
DRAWERS Clean drawers in bedroom/ kitchen/file cabinet.				
DRIVE Take the 55-Alive or similar defensive driving course.				

Topic	Interested?			Remarks
	Yes	No	Later	
DROMEDARY Ride/photograph a camel.				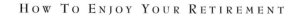
DUDE Visit a dude ranch.				
ECLECTIC Decorate with several styles of furniture.				
ECLIPSE Watch/study/travel to see the next eclipse.				
EGYPTOLOGY Study antiquities of Egypt.				
ELECTRICITY Study electricity.				
ELIZABETHAN Study Elizabeth I of England.				
EMBROIDER Learn to embroider.				
EMMY Watch Emmy awards on TV.				
ENGLISH Help someone speak/read.				
ENVIRONMENTALIST Work to improve the environment.				

Topic	Interested?			Remarks
	Yes	No	Later	
LABORATORY Do scientific research.				
LACE Make lace; teach others how to make lace.				
LAITY Help out at your place of worship.				
LAMINATE Make layers of wood/plastic for woodcrafts, plaques, menus, maps, and ID cards.				
LANCELOT Act in a play/show.				
LAND FILL Complain about hazardous waste-dumping.				
LANDSCAPE Paint/photograph/landscape your yard.				
LANGUAGE Learn/teach a new language.				
LAP DOG Get a very small dog.				
LAUGH And the world laughs with you!				

Topic	Interested?			Remarks
	Yes	No	Later	
LAUNCHING PAD Build model rockets.				
LAYER CAKE Learn/teach how to bake/ decorate cakes.				
LEADERSHIP Train in/teach leadership skills.				
LEARN Learn a new skill/craft/ occupation/hobby.				
LECTURE Speak publicly about your favorite subject.				
LEGISLATION Monitor the state legislature.				
LEPRECHAUN Study Irish folklore.				
LETTERS Write praise/complaint letters to companies.				
LIP READ Learn/teach lip reading.				
LIVEN UP Liven up your own or someone else's life.				

Topic	Interested?			Remarks
	Yes	No	Later	
LOAF Spend some time lazily.				
LOBSTER Cook lobster; invite friends.				
LUFTWAFFE Learn about the German Air Force in WWII.				
LUGGAGE Pack up and go somewhere you want to see.				
LURE Make your own fishing lures; try them out.				
MACBETH Read Shakespeare.				
MAGIC Perform magic tricks.				
MAH-JONGG Learn to play this Chinese game.				
MALAPROPISM Misuse words; send examples to *Reader's Digest*.				
MAMBO Learn this rumba-like dance.				

Topic	Interested?			Remarks
	Yes	No	Later	
MANUSCRIPT Write that steamy novel.				
MARKSMAN Practice sport shooting.				
MARXISM/LENINISM Study history/politics of Germany/Russia.				
MASTERMIND Plan/execute a project skillfully.				
MASTER OF CEREMONY Preside over entertainment or dinner.				
MAYA Visit a Mayan temple.				
MAYFLOWER Learn about the pilgrims.				
MAYOR Run for mayor.				
MECHANIC Fix things for yourself/others.				
MEMORY Improve your memory/ concentration.				
MENTAL RETARDATION Work with people with mental retardation.				

Topic	Interested?			Remarks
	Yes	No	Later	
MENTOR Be a mentor/guide to someone.				
MILE Walk a mile or two every day.				
MILKY WAY Learn/teach about the solar system.				
MIME Narrate without words (pantomime).				
MINCE PIE Enter your favorite recipe in a contest/fair.				
MONOCHROME Paint or draw in a single color.				
MORSE CODE Learn/teach Morse code.				
MUSICIAN Learn to play a/another musical instrument.				
MUZZLE LOADER Collect antique firearms.				
NAACP Work for organizations devoted to advancing the rights of people of color.				

Topic	Interested?			Remarks
	Yes	No	Later	
NAP It's okay to take a nap after retirement (and even before!).				
NARRATE Tell stories to someone.				
NATIVE AMERICAN Study the history and culture of a tribe.				
NATURAL HISTORY Study animals/plants/minerals.				
NATURAL RESOURCE Work to protect soil/forests/ endangered species/water.				
NATURE Study the physical universe and its phenomena.				
NAUTICAL Study ships/sailors/navigation.				
NEGOTIATE Bargain for what you want.				
NEIGHBOR Meet and make friends with neighbors.				
NESTOR Read what this wise old king did in the Trojan War.				

HOW TO ENJOY YOUR RETIREMENT

Topic	Interested?			Remarks
	Yes	No	Later	
NETWORK Build a support network of friends/associates/helpers; use/ join a computer network such as America Online or Prodigy.				
NEUROLOGY Study the nervous system.				
NEW DEAL Study President F. D. Roosevelt's policies.				
NEW/OLD TESTAMENT Take a Bible study class.				
NEW ZEALAND Study/visit New Zealand.				
NICKEL Start a coin collection.				
NICKELODEON Buy/repair/collect jukeboxes.				
NIRVANA Learn about the ideals and goal of Buddhism.				
NOCTURNAL Study animals/flowers that come out at night.				
NOISE Learn about noise stress and reduce yours.				

Topic	Interested?			Remarks
	Yes	No	Later	
NONVOTER Convince a nonvoter to vote.				
NORSE Study Scandinavian culture.				
NORTHUMBRIA Study ancient Anglo-Saxon Britain.				
NORTH VIETNAM Study the causes/effects of the Vietnam War.				
NOTE Learn to read music.				
NOUGAT Make this candy with honey, and pistachios.				
NOVELTY Manufacture/sell trinkets.				
NUCLEAR ENERGY Learn about this energy alternative; stand for or against.				
NUDISM Investigate this philosophy — is it for you?				
NURSE Become a nurse; help someone who is ill.				

 HOW TO ENJOY YOUR RETIREMENT

Topic	Interested?			Remarks
	Yes	No	Later	
NURSING HOME Visit/entertain the elderly.				
NUTRITION Study nutrition; eat properly.				
OBEDIENCE Take your dog to obedience school.				
OBERON Study medieval folklore.				
OBITUARY Write/call people before you find their names in the obituary.				
OBSERVE Take time to see/enjoy your world.				
OCELOT Visit a zoo or natural history museum.				
OCTET Play in a group of eight musical performers.				
OCTOPUS Study marine life.				
ODIN Study Norse mythology.				

Topic	Interested?			Remarks
	Yes	No	Later	
ODYSSEY Read/enjoy Homer's epic poem.				
OIL Follow/buy some oil stock.				
OIL PAINT Try this easy form of painting.				
OLD WORLD Visit Europe or Asia				
OLYMPIC GAMES Attend/watch/work for the Olympic Games.				
OMELET Make eggs folded over something tasty.				
OPAL Study/sell/collect gems.				
OP ART Study 1960s art and geometric/ optical illusions.				
OPEN-HEARTED Be candid and kind.				
OPERA Enjoy an opera/operetta.				
OPPORTUNITY Be open/ready when oppor- tunity knocks.				

Topic	Interested?			Remarks
	Yes	No	Later	
OPTIMISM Keep a cheerful attitude.				
ORCHARD Grow fruit/nut/olive trees.				
ORCHESTRA Play in/listen to an orchestra.				
ORCHID Raise orchids; enter contests; join a society.				
ORIENT Visit/study/invest in Asia/the East.				
ORION Study constellations and mythology.				
OROGENY Study the process of mountain formation.				
ORPHEUS Read about him in Greek mythology.				
ORWELLIAN Read the writings of satirist George Orwell.				
OSPREY Observe/study this large hawk that feeds on fish.				

Topic	Interested?			Remarks
	Yes	No	Later	
OSTEOLOGY Study the functions of bones.				
OTTER Observe/learn about this swimming mammal with webbed feet.				
OUIJA Play on the board/spell out telepathic messages.				
OUTBOARD Buy/ride in a motorboat.				
OUTDOORS Enjoy the great outdoors.				
OXTAIL Buy one and make soup.				
OXYMORON Use/create combinations of contradictory words.				
OYSTER Enjoy fresh oysters/oyster stew.				
OZONE Learn about the upper atmosphere.				
PAGODA Visit the Far East; see a tower used as a temple.				

 HOW TO ENJOY YOUR RETIREMENT

Topic	Interested?			Remarks
	Yes	No	Later	
PAINT Paint rooms/houses/pictures.				
PALESTINE Study the history/politics of Palestine.				
PALETTE KNIFE Mix and apply artist's colors.				
PALMISTRY Read the past/future in the palm of your hand.				
PAMPHLET Write/distribute political pamphlets.				
PANAMA CANAL Take a trip through the canal.				
PANEL DISCUSSION Moderate/participate in a panel discussion.				
PANELING Remove paneling; panel a wall.				
PANORAMA Enjoy/photograph/paint a lovely view.				
PANSY Grow pansies.				

Topic	Interested?			Remarks
	Yes	No	Later	
PAPACY Study the Roman Catholic government.				
PAPER HANGER Paper some walls; hang wallpaper borders.				
PAR Play golf with friends.				
PARACHUTE Did you have a golden one?				
PARADE Design/build/ride on parade floats.				
PARAGRAPH Your novel/letter begins with the paragraph.				
PARAKEET Buy a parakeet/parrot.				
PARAPSYCHOLOGY Study telepathy/ESP/psychic phenomena.				
PARI-MUTUEL Bet only what you can afford to lose.				
PARK Walk in/help build a park.				

Topic	Interested?			Remarks
	Yes	No	Later	
PARKINSON'S DISEASE Help someone with this disease.				
PARQUET Install some inlaid woodwork.				
PARTHENON See the Acropolis at Athens.				
PASTA Make/eat pasta; open an Italian restaurant.				
PASTEL Draw with colored pencils.				
PASTE-UP Publish a newsletter.				
PATROL Ride along with the police/ sheriff/fire department.				
PAUNCH Watch that waistline.				
PEARL Dive for pearls; make pearl jewelry.				
PEDDLE Sell small wares.				
PEDICURE Care for your own/someone else's feet.				

Topic	Interested?			Remarks
	Yes	No	Later	
PEDIGREE Buy/show/raise purebred dogs.				
PENITENTIARY Visit a prison.				
PENMANSHIP Teach penmanship; write letters for someone.				
PENTATHLON Enter an athletic contest of five events.				
PERIODIC TABLE Study chemistry.				
PERSUASION Practice the art of persuasion.				
PETROGRAPHY Describe and classify rocks.				
PEWTER Make/collect pewter figures.				
PHAETON Ride in/buy an early, open, two-seat automobile.				
PHARMACOLOGY Study the uses/effects of drugs.				
PHILATELY Collect postage stamps and stamped envelopes.				

Topic	Interested?			Remarks
	Yes	No	Later	
PHOBIA Study/try hypnotism as therapy for fears.				
PHONICS Teach spelling/reading using phonics.				
PHONOGRAPH Tape your old phonograph records.				
PHYSICAL EDUCATION Train/develop athletes.				
PHYSICAL THERAPY Make use of ice/heat/massage/exercise/rest.				
PHYSIOGNOMY Study how facial features reveal character.				
PIANO/KEYBOARD Learn to entertain yourself/others.				
PICTOGRAPH Draw a picture representing an idea.				
PIG Get a cute little piggy for a pet.				
PIGEON Raise/race pigeons.				

Topic	Interested?			Remarks
	Yes	No	Later	
PILGRIMAGE Go on a pilgrimage.				
PILOT Learn to fly a plane.				
PINEAPPLE Make a fancy dish with fresh pineapple.				
PINECONE Make a holiday decoration/ wreath.				
PINOCHLE Play this great card game.				
PIPE DREAM Daydreaming is okay.				
PITCHMAN Sell small articles at a fair.				
PIZZAZZ Live life with flair/irresistible charm.				
PLAID Study plaids of the Scottish Highlands.				
PLAN Make plans for your day, week, and year and for a special event.				

Topic	Interested?			Remarks
	Yes	No	Later	
PLANET Study the planets/universe.				
PLANTAGENET Study the British royal family from Henry II to the Tudor era.				
PLASTER OF PARIS Make molds/statuary/train layout.				
PLAYHOUSE Build a playhouse for kids.				
PLEASE Please yourself/your significant other.				
PLUMBING Repair your plumbing.				
POETRY Read/write/enjoy poetry.				
POINSETTIA Try to get one to turn red again.				
POKER Enjoy playing cards with friends.				
POLAND Learn the language/travel to Poland.				

Topic	Interested?			Remarks
	Yes	No	Later	
POLARIS Study the star that stays in fixed position.				
POLISH Polish your furniture/car.				
POLKA Learn/enjoy the polka.				
POLL Take a poll or census.				
POLO Try this game on horseback.				
POMOLOGY Study the science of fruit culture.				
POOL Swim for fun and relaxation; shoot pool with friends; pool funds and splurge.				
POP ART Study painting that looks like comic strips.				
PORK BARREL Monitor spending in the legislature.				
POSITIVE Maintain a positive attitude.				

Topic	Interested?			Remarks
	Yes	No	Later	
PRETZEL Enjoy a chewy, plump, warm one with a cold beer or soda pop.				
PULSE Take someone's pulse for them.				
PUPPET Put on a puppet show.				
PURL Learn to knit and purl.				
PURSUE Do something you always wanted to do.				
PUTTER Putter around the house and yard.				
PUZZLE Work puzzles to keep your mind alert.				
PYRAMID Study the Egyptian pyramids.				
QUADRILLE Learn/teach a square dance for four couples.				
QUAIL Hunt/eat quail.				

Topic	Interested?			Remarks
	Yes	No	Later	
QUAKER Learn about the Society of Friends.				
QUARREL Mend a quarrel if you can.				
QUARTET Play instruments/sing with three other people.				
QUICHE Make a meat, cheese, or vegetable quiche.				
QUICKSTEP Learn to dance the quickstep.				
QUICK-WITTED Enjoy a keen, alert, ready wit.				
QUIET Arrange to have some peace and quiet.				
QUIZ PROGRAM Match wits with contestants.				
QUOTATIONS Collect wonderful quotations.				
RACKET Play tennis.				

Topic	Interested?			Remarks
	Yes	No	Later	
RACONTEUR Become a skilled storyteller.				
RAILROAD Collect/trade/sell model trains.				
RAIN GAUGE Keep a weather diary.				
RANCH Visit a dude ranch.				
RANGER Volunteer as a forest ranger.				
RAPIER Learn to duel.				
RASPBERRY Grow raspberries/make preserves.				
RAVIOLI Make some, or order at an Italian restaurant.				
RAZE Tear down that old shed.				
READ Read anything and everything.				
RECIPE Try new recipes; enter contests.				

Topic	Interested?			Remarks
	Yes	No	Later	
RECITAL Attend/give a recital.				
RECLAIM Bring back a vacant lot/ swamp or other area.				
RECONCILE Revive friendship after a quarrel.				
RECREATION Refresh your body/mind.				
RED CROSS Volunteer for the Red Cross.				
RED-HOT Get excited about a new idea.				
RED SNAPPER Catch/cook/eat red snapper.				
REEL Reel in that big fish; dance one, Virginia.				
REFEREE Act as referee for sports events.				
REFRESHER COURSE Take a class at community college.				
REJOIN Reunite with old friends/clubs.				

Topic	Interested?			Remarks
	Yes	No	Later	
REMINISCE Remember the good times.				
REPRESENTATIVE Know what your politicians are doing.				
RESTAURANT Open one if you're a good cook.				
RETREAT Buy/rent one; go on a religious retreat.				
REUNION Plan a family/class/military reunion.				
REVEL Rejoice in your new-found freedom.				
REWARD Feel satisfied with what you do/have/own.				
RICH Beware of get-rich-quick schemes.				
RIFLE Hunt with/collect firearms.				
RINGER Join a group of bell ringers, or play horseshoes.				

Topic	Interested?			Remarks
	Yes	No	Later	
RINSE Cover gray hair with a rinse.				
RIPSAW Work with wood; finish your basement.				
RIVER Take a cruise on a riverboat.				
ROAST Plan a roast for a friend.				
ROBIN Enjoy/feed/study/photograph/watch birds.				
ROCKING CHAIR You're not ready for one yet.				
ROCKING HORSE Build one for your grand-children.				
SADDLE Take a horseback ride.				
SAILING How about a nice sailboat ride?				
SALMON Grill and serve with cucumber sauce.				

Topic	Interested?			Remarks
	Yes	No	Later	
SALVATION ARMY Work for/donate to the Salvation Army.				
SANTA FE TRAIL Ride the trade route from Independence, MO.				
SAPLING Plant a tree to commemorate a special event.				
SAXOPHONE Learn to play and enjoy.				
SCOUTING Become a leader in the Boy/ Girl Scouts.				
SCUBA DIVE Visit colorful fish in lovely warm water.				
SERENDIPITY Notice fortunate discoveries made by accident.				
SHELF Build shelves where needed.				
SHINGLE Check/repair your roof.				
SHIP Take a cruise. Collect/build model ships.				

Topic	Interested?			Remarks
	Yes	No	Later	
SHRUBBERY Trim your shrubs/trees/garden.				
SHUTTLECOCK Play badminton.				
SKYDIVE How about jumping out of an airplane?				
SKYLIGHT Install a skylight; remodel your home.				
SLEUTH Read/write a good mystery.				
SMOKE Quit smoking—again.				
SNOWSHOE Try snowshoeing.				
SOCCER Play/coach soccer.				
SOCRATIC METHOD Learn about this method of instruction.				
SOLDER Make, repair, or connect something metal.				
SONG Sing/write/play a song.				

Topic	Interested?			Remarks
	Yes	No	Later	
SPAY Work to get animals spayed and neutered.				
SPEAR THROWING Enter a spear-throwing contest.				
SPEECH Take a speech class; join Toastmasters.				
SPEEDBOAT Take a ride in a speedboat.				
SPELUNKER Explore/study caves.				
SPORTSWEAR Trade in your business suit.				
SQUEAK Fix squeaks; squeaking wheel gets greased.				
STAINED GLASS Try your hand at this art form.				
STAND-IN Be a stand-in for the star of the show.				
STARGAZE Gaze at/study the stars; daydream.				

Topic	Interested?			Remarks
	Yes	No	Later	
STAR-SPANGLED BANNER Write a new national anthem.				
STATISTICIAN Collect/tabulate statistical data.				
STEPPINGSTONE Place steppingstones in your garden.				
STOCKBROKER Monitor your portfolio closely.				
STOCK CAR Build/race a stock car.				
STONE AGE Study cultural evolution and/or stone implements.				
STOPWATCH Help out as a timer at athletic events.				
STRETCH Do stretching exercises; keep flexible.				
SUICIDE Work a suicide hot line.				
SUNRISE Watch/paint/photograph the sunrise/sunset.				

Topic	Interested?			Remarks
	Yes	No	Later	
SUPERMARKET Share the shopping.				
SUPERNATURAL Study phenomena beyond the known laws of nature.				
SURVEILLANCE Become a brilliant private investigator.				
SURVEY Do a survey in your area.				
SWIM Swim for fun/exercise.				
SWISS Visit Switzerland; open a Swiss bank account.				
TABERNACLE Volunteer at your place of worship.				
TABLE TENNIS Play ping pong.				
TACO Make a Mexican dinner; invite friends.				
TAILOR Make/repair garments.				

Topic	Interested?			Remarks
	Yes	No	Later	
TALENT Use all your talents.				
TALK Talk to everyone you meet.				
TALMUD Study Jewish civil/religious law.				
TANDEM Ride a bicycle built for two.				
TANGO Learn this beautiful Latin dance.				
TAX Prepare taxes for others.				
TAXICAB Drive a taxi in your spare time.				
TAXIDERMY Stuff/mount animals/fish.				
TEDDY BEAR Study the history of/collect teddy bears.				
TEENAGE Work with teens.				
TELEPATHY Study/practice mind communication.				

Topic	Interested?			Remarks
	Yes	No	Later	
TELEPHONE Phone your friends often.				
TIME CLOCK You don't have to punch a time clock now.				
TRACTOR Collect/swap/trade toy farm implements.				
TRAIN Collect toy trains; build layouts.				
TRANSLATE Help someone with foreign languages.				
TRAVEL Travel where you've always wanted to go.				
TRAVELOGUE Speak about/show slides of your trip.				
TRICEPS Exercise with weights.				
TRICYCLE Buy a tricycle for your grandchild.				
TROJAN WAR Study the ten-year war.				

Topic	Interested?			Remarks
	Yes	No	Later	
TROPIC Fly off to the tropics.				
TROPICAL FISH Have a beautiful aquarium.				
TROUT Fish in the mountains.				
TROWEL Learn to lay bricks.				
TUNE-UP Get/give your car a tune-up.				
TURKEY Fix a turkey dinner and invite friends.				
TUTOR Be a tutor to someone.				
TUTU Take kids to ballet lessons/a recital.				
UFO Study unidentified flying objects.				
UKRAINIAN Learn about/visit the Ukraine.				
UKULELE Take lessons on the ukulele.				

Topic	Interested?			Remarks
	Yes	No	Later	
UMBRELLA Buy a new umbrella for your picnic table or golf cart.				
UMPIRE Act as umpire for a ballgame.				
UNDERGROUND RAILROAD Learn about antislavery efforts and advocates.				
UNDERSTUDY Stand in for an actor.				
UNESCO Work for the United Nations Educational, Scientific, and Cultural Organization.				
UNICYCLE Ride a single-wheel vehicle.				
UPHOLSTERY Study covering furniture with fabric; redo your chair/sofa.				
URSA MAJOR/MINOR Study astronomy.				
USHER Usher at your place of worship.				
VACATION Take a vacation. You've earned it.				

Topic	Interested?			Remarks
	Yes	No	Later	
VACCINATE Work to vaccinate children/ pets.				
VENEREAL DISEASE Counsel young people on venereal disease.				
VIETNAM Learn about the history/culture of Vietnam.				
VOCABULARY Improve your vocabulary.				
VOCALIST Sing at services/events/parties.				
VOLUNTEER Volunteer at a school/hospital/ nursing home.				
WALK Walk for fun/exercise.				
WAR GAME Play war games with friends.				
WAR PLANE Build/collect models of war planes.				
WATCHMAKER Repair watches; build clocks.				

Topic	Interested?			Remarks
	Yes	No	Later	
WATERCOLOR Paint with watercolors.				
WATERLOO Learn about Napoleon's defeat.				
WEATHER-STRIP Apply weather stripping around windows/doors.				
WEAVE Learn to weave baskets/paper/ cloth.				
WEDGWOOD Collect pottery of white cameo on tinted background.				
WHALE Learn about whales; travel to see them.				
WHEELER-DEALER Become one: buy/sell/trade.				
WHIRLPOOL Get into a hot tub.				
WHISKEY Enjoy a toddy before dinner.				
WHITE HOUSE Learn about its present and past residents and furnishings.				

Topic	Interested?			Remarks
	Yes	No	Later	
WHITTLE Turn scraps of wood into toys/figures/useful items.				
WHODUNIT Read/write a good mystery.				
WILDERNESS Enjoy being in the wilderness.				
WILD WEST Study the early history of the American West.				
WIND GAUGE Study/record/report weather conditions.				
WINDSOR Learn about the British royal family.				
WITCH DOCTOR Learn about the medical/spiritual practices of this professional in some societies.				
WOK Cook with this Chinese pan.				
WOODWIND Play a wind instrument.				
WORK OF ART See works of art; create your own.				

Topic	Interested?			Remarks
	Yes	No	Later	
WORKOUT Maintain physical fitness skills/routine.				
WORKSHOP Create a space where you can work.				
WORLD SERIES Enjoy the World Series.				
WORLD WAR I and II Study the two world wars.				
WRESTLING Teach/coach wrestling; wrestle your worries to the ground.				
XENOGAMY Learn/teach about cross pollination between flowers on different plants.				
XENOPHOBIA Study about fear of strangers or foreigners.				
XEROPHYTE Study plants structurally adapted for life with limited water.				
XYLOGRAPHY Study artistic wood carving.				

Topic	Interested?			Remarks
	Yes	No	Later	
XYLOPHONE Learn to play the xylophone.				
YACHT Buy/rent a yacht for a trip.				
YELLOW Appreciate yellow birds, plants, bushes, trees.				
YEW Plant a yew tree.				
YIDDISH Study the Yiddish language.				
YIN/YANG Study Chinese philosophy.				
YODEL Learn to yodel.				
YOGA Take/teach a yoga class for body and mind.				
YORKSHIRE Make a batter pudding and bake it in meat drippings, then invite a guest to help eat it.				
ZEBRA See a zebra at a zoo.				

Topic	Interested?			Remarks
	Yes	No	Later	
ZEN Pursue enlightenment through meditation.				
ZEPPELIN Study airships manufactured by Count Ferdinand von Zeppelin, circa 1910.				
ZINNIA Plant zinnias in your garden.				
ZIRCONIUM Buy a nice item of zirconium jewelry.				
ZITHER Learn to play a zither; play the Third Man Theme.				
ZODIAC Study the signs of the zodiac.				
ZOIC Study geological eras: Archeozoic, Mesozoic, Paleozoic, and Cenozoic eras.				
ZOOM Make pictures more interesting by zooming in or out with your camera/camcorder.				
ZYMURGY Make and enjoy homemade wine or beer.				

APPENDIX A

· ·

PERSONAL INVENTORY

Who Are You?

Name

Ancestors

Countries of origin

Are you interested in studying your ancestors (genealogy), their countries of origin, or their languages? Do you want to visit these countries?

Living relatives (mother/father, brothers/sisters, uncles/aunts, cousins)

Do you want to know any relatives better? Would you like to have a family reunion?

Do you want to find/reunite with someone?

Do any relationships need repair? When/how?

Religion/faith

Are you pleased with your current level of involvement in religious activities/community? If no, what do you want to change? When?

Are you physically active? If so, what sports/activities do you enjoy?

Do you have any hobbies (e.g., stamp collecting, cooking, gardening)? If so, what are they?

Do you enjoy any crafts (e.g., needlecraft, woodworking, tole painting, sewing)? If so, what crafts do you enjoy?

Do you enjoy playing card games and/or board games (e.g., bridge, mah-jongg, Scrabble)? If so, what games do you enjoy?

Do you belong to clubs or fraternal organizations so that you have "buddies" to do things with?

Do you have close friends? Have your friendships been affected or will they be affected by your retirement?

Are you involved in your community? How involved do you want to be?

What Have You Done?
What Do You Do Well?

Occupation(s)

Talents, languages, skills

Past successes

If you went to college, what did you like to do?

    Offices held

    Accomplishments

While in high school, what did you like to do?

    Offices held

    Accomplishments

Do you sing, dance, or play an instrument?

Do you enjoy sports? As a spectator or participant? What are the sports you enjoy?

Do you enjoy doing things with your significant other? What are they?

When Will or Did You Retire?

Age

    Early retirement?

    Retired from what/where?

    If you have not already retired, when (date) and at what age will you retire?

Is your significant other working? Retired? Has s/he always been home?

How will your significant other feel about having you home full-time?

Where Will You Live?

Will you stay in your present house/condo/apartment?

    Is it paid for? If it is not, how much do you still owe?

    Do you want a smaller or larger home?

    Is your yard too big, too small, just right?

Do you want to move? Where do you want to move?

    Do you mind shoveling snow?

    Do you enjoy winter sports such as skiing, skating, hockey?

    Do you want to live in a retirement community?

    Do you want to spend winters in a warm climate? If yes, in what state?

    Do you want to be near or away from your children or grandchildren?

Is travel in your plans?

Have you traveled extensively, a little, or never?

Do you own a motorhome or camper?

Why Are You Retiring?

Are you retiring due to age?

Are you taking early retirement?

Are you "fed up" with working?

Are you retiring due to illness?

Is there another reason for your retirement? If so, what?

Who, if anyone, will rely on you for assistance of some kind after you retire?

Do your parents need help?

Does your brother/sister need help?

Do your children or grandchildren need help?

Is there anyone else relying on you?

How do you feel about retirement? What do you expect it to be?

How Will You Pay for Retirement?

Will you have—

a regular (steady) income?

a retirement check?

Social Security? If not now, when?

investment returns?

Do you *need* to work? Full-time or part-time?

Do you *want* to work? Full-time or part-time?

What are your obligations or debts?

House payment/rent

Car payment

Utilities

Food

Credit cards

Other

Can you live on your retirement income, social security, IRAs, and investments (stocks, bonds, annuities)?

How much more do you need or want?

Do you want to enjoy freedom, leisure, travel?

Do you want to start a business of some kind?

Determining Your Net Worth

Assets

Cash (checking and savings accounts)

Securities (stocks and bonds)

Mutual funds

Receivables (loans made, rebates)

Life insurance cash value

Jewelry, art, and antiques (current market value)

Automobiles (current market value)

Retirement accounts

Pension lump-sum value

Home (current market value)

Other real estate (current market value)

Other assets (collections, furniture, appliances; current market value)

Total

Liabilities

Current bills (rent, telephone, electric, gas)

Credit-card debt

Taxes payable

Auto loans

Installment loans

Home mortgage

Home-equity loan

Student loans

Other liabilities (child care, parent care)

Total

Net Worth

Total Assets minus *Total Liabilities* equals *Net Worth*

HOW TO ENJOY YOUR RETIREMENT

APPENDIX B

. . . .

SPENDING TIME WITH GRANDCHILDREN

Time spent with children can be richly rewarding. We are calling them grandchildren in this book, but they could be nieces, nephews, neighbors, or any children you are lucky enough to be around. You'll enjoy yourself, and the children will have some very special memories of you.

ACTIVITIES

Fun activities might include taking your grandchildren on outings. These do not have to be expensive: visit a library; take a nature walk; go to zoos and museums during times of free or reduced admission. Yearly memberships at nearby attractions are a bargain if you visit often. You can also share your own interests and skills with your grandchildren—anything from fixing cars to birdwatching to playing an instrument or a sport. Teach your grandchildren songs and dances from your native heritage, and cook old country dishes together. Travel with them. Teach older children about money management—saving, budgeting, investing, etc. Libraries and bookstores offer books full of ideas for activities to do with children, and we'll bet you have a few ideas of your own.

> *Never have children, only grandchilden.*
>
> —Gore Vidal

Brain Gym—Do whole-brain exercises with your grandchildren. These fun exercises show that movement and learning can work together. Refer to Appendix C for sample *Brain Gym* activities.

Classics Illustrated Comics — Introduce your grandchild to *Classics Illustrated* comics. Acclaim Books is reissuing the entire *Classics Illustrated* lineup in a digest-sized book. Check your local bookstore.

Fun with Science and Nature — Buy one of a series of books by Janice VanCleave (John Wiley & Sons, $12.95 each), including *Play and Find Out about Nature* for ages 4–7 and *200 Gooey, Slippery, Slimey, Weird, and Fun Experiments*. The second book includes a wacky recipe for green glob goop that you make with white school glue, green food coloring, distilled water, and 20-Mule Team borax powder. Then you use the glob in experiments that demonstrate some properties of physics and fluids. Gather up some children and have a ball turning them on to science. VanCleave's books have special sections to refresh your knowledge of science basics.

Money Management — Turn a common practice such as grocery shopping into a learning activity. Get the free guidebook *Kids, Cash, Plastic, and You* from Consumer Information Center, Pueblo, CO 81009 (1-719-948-4000).

Travel with Kids — Read *Great Nature Vacations with Your Kids* and *Great Adventure Vacations with Your Kids* by Dorothy Jordan (World Leisure Corp., $9.95 and $11.95, telephone 1-800-444-2524). We also recommend *Family Camping Made Simple* and *RV Camping with Children* by Beverly Liston (Globe Pequot Press, $12.95 each).

BABY-SITTING HELP

Choking Hazards — Balloons are the single most dangerous, nonfood choking item for children under three and as old as eleven. Also watch out for marbles, for coins, and for toys with small detachable parts. Any object that can pass through a toilet-paper tube is too small for a child under three to play with. Window treatment and drapery cords also present a choking hazard. You can convert two-corded miniblinds and wood blinds to safer models by contacting 3-Day Blinds at 1-800-800-3DAY (800-3329) for a retail location near you. They allow up to ten free conversion kits per customer.

Sudden Infant Death Syndrome (SIDS) — Studies have shown that placing a baby to sleep on its back is safer than laying it on its stomach.

Stimulate a Baby's Brain — Be warm, loving, and responsive to the child. Help build attachments. Talk, read, and sing to the child. Establish rituals and routines. Encourage safe exploration and play. Make television viewing selective. Use discipline calmly and as an opportunity to teach. Recognize that each child is unique and grows at an individual rate.

Car Safety — Place car seats in the back seat to avoid airbag injuries to children. No children should ever ride in the front seat of a car with airbags. The middle of the back seat is the safest place for a child to ride.

EDUCATING CHILDREN

If you plan to help children with schoolwork, to get involved with their education, or to volunteer in a classroom, the following information and resources could be useful. The information below is excerpted from "Each child learns in a different way, educators finding" by Carol Kreck, an article that appeared in the *Denver Post*, 1 September 1994.

> The book *Hassle-Free Homework*, written by Cecil Clark and Faith Clark with Marta Vogel (Doubleday, $18.95), explains how children learn in different ways. Certain characteristics indicate different learning modes, styles, or strengths, as described below.
>
> • **Visual External:** Sensitive to visual environment; learns by watching; likes movies and museums; is good at arranging objects, keeps the room straight.
>
> • **Visual Internal:** Makes pictures in head; recalls how things look; likes descriptive novels.

- **Auditory External:** Learns by listening; can listen to two conversations at once; especially sensitive to sound; sorts by how things sound.

- **Auditory Internal:** Hears words in head; recalls melodies; talks things over with self; recalls sounds of different voices.

- **Kinesthetic External:** Likes dancing, sports; likes to use hands; learns by doing.

- **Kinesthetic Internal:** Sorts by feelings; has strong body reactions to experiences; learns only when physically comfortable.

Harvard professor Howard Gardner discusses the theory of multiple intelligences in his books *Frames of Mind* (Basic Books, $16.50) and *The Unschooled Mind* (Basic Books, $16.00). He names seven intelligences, as follows:

- **Logical/Mathematical:** The ability to handle chains of reasoning and to recognize patterns. Typical of philosophers, mathematicians, scientists.

- **Linguistic:** Sensitivity to the meaning and order of words. Typical of poets, translators, historians, comedians, public speakers.

- **Musical:** The ability to produce and appreciate rhythm, melody, pitch, and tone. Typical of composers, singers.

- **Spatial:** The ability to perceive the visual world accurately and to recreate or modify aspects of that world. Typical of sculptors, architects, artists, surveyors.

- **Bodily/Kinesthetic:** The ability to control one's body movements and to handle objects skillfully. Typical of athletes, dancers, surgeons.

- **Interpersonal:** The ability to discern and respond appropriately to the temperaments and motivations of other people. Typical of politicians, teachers, salespersons, religious leaders, entrepreneurs.

- **Intrapersonal:** The ability to access one's own strengths, weaknesses, desires, and intelligences as a means to understand oneself and others. Typical of psychologists, therapists, social workers.

Bernice McCarthy of Excel, Inc., in Oak Brook, Illinois, developed a method for grouping students according to four learning styles.

- **Innovative Learners:** Seek meaning; need to be personally involved; learn by listening and sharing ideas; interested in people and culture; divergent thinkers who excel in viewing concrete situations from many perspectives; favorite question—"Why/Why not?"; learn by sensing, feeling, and watching. (Likely to excel in counseling, humanities, organizational development.)

- **Analytic Learners:** Seek facts; need to know what the experts think; less interested in people than in concepts; enjoy traditional classrooms; favorite question—"What?"; learn by watching and thinking. (Likely to excel in basic sciences, math, research, planning.)

- **Common Sense Learners:** Need to know how things work; learn by testing theories in ways that seem reasonable; have limited tolerance for "fuzzy ideas"; need hands-on experience; favorite question—"How does this work?"; learn by thinking and doing. (Likely to exceed in engineering, physical sciences, nursing, technical support positions.)

- **Dynamic Learners:** Seek hidden possibilities; learn by trial and error; adaptable to change; function by acting and testing experience; favorite question—"What can this become?"; learn by doing, sensing, and feeling. (Likely to exceed in marketing, sales, action-oriented managerial jobs.)

Adam Robinson is the author of several books on education. You may want to read one or more of them. His titles include *What Smart Students Know* (Crown, $16.00), *Word Smart II: How to Build a More Educated Vocabulary* (Villard Books, $12.00), and with Mertz and others: *Cracking the GMAT, . . . the GRE, . . . the SAT and PSAT,* and so on (Princeton Review, various prices).

APPENDIX C

BRAIN GYM® ACTIVITIES

This appendix contains five sample activities from the book *Brain Gym Teacher's Edition. Brain Gym* exercises can be applied to any academic skill; visual, mental, or physical task; or performance activity. They are designed to draw out the learner's innate gifts and talents, to reduce stresses and disabilities, and to bring about whole-brain learning. *Brain Gym* can be used by people of all ages. Give it a try. You may want to buy one of the books listed at the end of this paragraph or contact *Brain Gym's* headquarters for the name of an approved instructor or consultant near you. The books are written by Dr. Paul E. Dennison and Gail E. Dennison, directors of the Educational Kinesiology Foundation. The cost of *Brain Gym* is $9.00. The *Brain Gym Teacher's Edition* is $16.95. Write to Edu-Kinesthetics, Inc., P.O. Box 3395, Ventura, CA 93006-3395 or call 1-800-356-2109.

Arm Activation

ILLUSTRATION © LENICE STROHMEIER

Arm Activation is an isometric self-help activity which lengthens the muscles of the upper chest and shoulders. Muscular control for both gross-motor and fine-motor activities originates in this area. If these muscles are shortened from tension, activities related to writing and the control of tools are inhibited.

Teaching Tips

• The student experiences her arms as they hang loosely at her sides.

- The student activates one arm as illustrated [on previous page], while keeping her head relaxed. She then compares the two arms in terms of length, relaxation, and flexibility, before activating the other arm.

- Activation is done in four positions; away from the head, forward, backward, and toward the ear.

- The student may feel the arm activation all the way down to the ribcage.

- The student exhales on the activation, releasing the breath over eight or more counts.

- The student may notice increased relaxation, coordination, and vitality as arm tension is released.

- On completing the movement, the student rolls or shakes her shoulders, noticing the relaxation.

Variations

- Take more than one complete breath in each position of activation.

- While activating, reach up to further open the diaphragm.

- This can be done sitting, standing, or lying down.

- Arm Activations can be done in different arm positions (e.g., arm straight ahead, next to hip, behind the waist).

Activates the Brain For

- expressive speech and language ability
- relaxed use of diaphragm and increased respiration
- eye-hand coordination and the manipulation of tools

Academic Skills

- penmanship and cursive writing
- spelling
- creating writing

Related Skills

- operating machines (e.g., a word processor)

Brain Gym® is a registered trademark of the Educational Kinesiology Foundation, Ventura, California (1-800-356-2109).

Behavioral/Postural Correlates

- an increased attention span for written work
- improved focus and concentration without overfocus
- improved breathing and a relaxed attitude
- an enhanced ability to express ideas
- increased energy in hands and fingers (relaxes writer's cramp)

Balance Buttons

ILLUSTRATION © LENICE STROHMEIER

The Balance Buttons provide a quick balance for all three dimensions: left/right, top/bottom, and back/front. Restoring balance to the occiput [the back part of the head] and the inner-ear area helps to normalize the whole body. The student holds the Balance Buttons, located just above the indentation where the skull rests over the neck (about one and one-half to two inches to each side of the back midline) and just behind the mastoid area.

Teaching Tips

- The student holds one Balance Button while holding the navel with the other hand for about thirty seconds, then changes hands to hold the other Balance Button. The chin is tucked in; the head is level.
- Use two or more fingers to assure that the point is covered.
- Some people may experience a pulsation when the point is stimulated or held.

Variations

- Do the activity while standing, sitting, or lying down.

- Stimulate the points by massage before holding them.

- While holding the points, draw circles around a distant object with your nose, move your head from side to side, or look all around you, relaxing both eye and neck muscles.

- Press your head gently back into your fingers while holding the points, releasing neck tension or headache.

Activate the Brain For

- alertness and focus by stimulating the semicircular canals and reticular system
- decision-making, concentrating, and associative thinking
- changing visual focus from point to point
- increased proprioception [receptivity] for balance and equilibrium
- relaxed jaw and cranial movement

Academic Skills

- comprehension for "reading between the lines"
- perception of the author's point of view
- critical judgment and decision-making
- recognition skills for spelling and math

Related Skills

- report writing, reference work, phone or computer work
- release of motion sickness or of ear pressure built up at altitudes

Behavioral/Postural Correlates

- a sense of well-being
- an open and receptive attitude
- eyes, ears, and head more level on shoulders
- relaxation of an overfocused posture or attitude
- improved reflexes, including Cross Crawl ability

Brain Gym® is a registered trademark of the Educational Kinesiology Foundation, Ventura, California (1-800-356-2109).

Hook-Ups

ILLUSTRATION © LENICE STROHMEIER

Hook-ups connect the electrical circuits in the body, containing and thus focusing both attention and disorganized energy. The mind and body relax as energy circulates through areas blocked by tension. The figure 8 pattern of the arms and legs (Part One) follows the energy flow lines of the body. The touching of the fingertips (Part Two) balances and connects the two brain hemispheres.

Teaching Tips

• Part One: Sitting, the student crosses the left ankle over the right. He extends his arms before him, crossing the left wrist over the right. He then interlaces his fingers and draws his hands up toward his chest. He may now close his eyes, breathe deeply, and relax for about a minute. Optional: He presses his tongue flat against the roof of his mouth on inhalation, and relaxes the tongue on exhalation.

• Part Two: When ready, the student uncrosses his legs. He touches the fingertips of both hands together, continuing to breathe deeply for about another minute.

Variations

• Hook-ups may also be done while standing.

• Cook's Hook-ups, Part One: The student sits resting his left ankle on his right knee. He grasps his left ankle with his right hand, putting his left hand around the ball of the left foot (or shoe). He breathes deeply for about a minute, then continues with Part Two, as above.

• For Part One of any of the above versions, some people may prefer to place the right ankle and right wrist on top.

Activate the Brain For

- emotional centering
- grounding
- increased attention (stimulates reticular formation)
- cranial movement

Academic Skills

- clear listening and speaking
- test-taking and similar challenges
- work at the keyboard

Behavioral/Postural Correlates

- improved self-control and sense of boundaries
- improved balance and coordination
- increased comfort in the environment (less hypersensitivity)
- deeper respiration

The Owl

ILLUSTRATION © LENICE STROHMEIER

The bird for which this movement is named has a large head, large eyes, and soft feathers that enable it to fly noiselessly. The owl turns its head and eyes at the same time, and has an extremely full range of vision, as it can turn its head over 180 degrees. It also has radar-like hearing. The Owl movement addresses these same visual, auditory, and head-turning skills. The movement releases neck and shoulder tension that develops under stress, especially when

Brain Gym® is a registered trademark of the Educational Kinesiology Foundation, Ventura, California (1-800-356-2109).

holding a heavy book or when coordinating the eyes for reading or other near-point skills. Further, the Owl releases neck tension caused by subvocalization while reading. It lengthens neck and shoulder muscles, restoring range of motion and circulation of blood to the brain for improved focus, attention, and memory skills.

Teaching Tips

• The student squeezes one shoulder to release neck muscles tensed in reaction to listening, speaking, or thinking.

• The student moves his head smoothly across the midfield, to the left, then the right, keeping his chin level.

• The student exhales in each extended head position: to the left and then to the right, and again with the head tilted forward, to release back-of-the-neck muscles. The Owl is repeated with the other shoulder.

• The head may move further into the left and right auditory positions with each release.

Variations

• While doing the Owl, blink lightly, allowing eye movement to shift along the horizon.

• Add one or two complete breathing cycles in each of the three extended head positions, relaxing fully.

• Emphasize listening with the left ear (head left), right ear (head right), and both ears together (chin down).

• Make a sound (e.g., the owl's "who-o-o") on exhalation.

Activates the Brain For

• crossing the "auditory midline" (auditory attention, perception, and memory)

• listening to the sound of one's own voice

• short- and long-term memory

• silent speech and thinking ability

• efficient saccadic eye movement [the type used when reading]

• integration of vision and listening with whole-body movement

Academic Skills

• listening comprehension

• speech or oral reports

• mathematical computation

• memory (for spelling or digit spans)

• computer or other keyboard work

Behavioral/Postural Correlates

• the ability to turn the head left and right

• strength and balance of front and back neck muscles

• alleviated squinting or staring habits

• relaxed neck, jaw, and shoulder muscles, even when focusing

• head centering (helps release the need to tilt the head or lean on the elbows)

• balance front- and back-of-the-neck muscles (alleviates overfocused posture)

The Thinking Cap

This activity helps the student focus attention on his hearing. It also relaxes tension in the cranial bones. The student uses his thumbs and

index fingers to pull the ears gently back and unroll them. He begins at the top of the ear and gently massages down and around the curve, ending with the bottom lobe.

Teaching Tips

• The student keeps his head upright, chin comfortably level.

• The process may be repeated three or more times.

ILLUSTRATION © LENICE STROHMEIER

Brain Gym® is a registered trademark of the Educational Kinesiology Foundation, Ventura, California (1-800-356-2109).

Variations

• Include sounds (e.g., yawning sounds or vowel sounds).

• Do the movement while looking over a spelling list.

Activates the Brain For

• crossing the auditory midline (including auditory recognition, attention, discrimination, perception, memory)

• listening to one's own speaking voice

• short-term working memory

• silent speech and thinking skills

• increased mental and physical fitness

• hearing with both ears together

• switched-on reticular formation (screens out distracting sounds from relevant ones)

Academic Skills

• listening comprehension

• public speaking, singing, playing a musical instrument

• inner speech and verbal mediation

• spelling (decoding and encoding)

Related Skills

• mental arithmetic

• concentration while working with a computer or other electronic device

Behavioral/Postural Correlates

• improved breathing and energy

• increased voice resonance

• relaxed jaw, tongue, and facial muscles

• improved left-and-right head-turning ability

• enhanced focusing of the attention

• improved equilibrium, especially in a moving vehicle

• a better range of hearing

• expanded peripheral vision

APPENDIX D

. . . .

STARTING A BUSINESS:
SOURCES OF HELP AND INFORMATION

If you're planning to start a small business in the United States, the best source of free help and information is the Small Business Administration (SBA). The SBA is a small, independent, federal agency created to assist and counsel U.S. small businesses.

The Small Business Administration

The SBA has regional and district offices throughout the country, so look in your telephone book to see if there is an office in your town. Each SBA office provides free one-on-one counseling through its Senior Corps of Retired Executives (SCORE). The SBA offers a "Starter Kit," a publication called *How the SBA Can Help You Go into Business*, and a list of other publications (many of which are free). Write to the SBA at this address:

> U.S. Small Business Administration
> 1441 L Street
> Washington, DC 20416

The SBA in Texas distributes a series of management and technical publications for owner-managers and prospective owners of small businesses. Managers of small businesses can also order a free series of management aids (SBA115-A). Write to this address:

. . . .

SBA
P.O. Box 15434
Fort Worth, TX 76119

For-a-fee booklets are available to cover a wide range of business subjects. Get the list from the SBA (item SBA115-B), then order the ones you want by writing to this address:

Superintendent of Documents
U.S. Government Printing Office
Washington, DC 20402

The Superintendent of Documents also makes available a directory of SBA programs and activities. This lists every program and activity, by office, in the SBA.

The Consumer Information Center in Pueblo, Colorado (1-719-948-4000; address below) distributes almost twenty booklets and pamphlets, available at no cost or for a moderate sum. Many of these publications are aimed at people starting a business. In addition, the Consumer Information Center offers two other booklets: (1) *Starting and Managing a Small Service Business* (item 115V) is full of tips and tables to help you sort through business legalities, estimate costs, and track expenses; (2) the *Directory of Business Development Publications* (item 581V) is a listing of SBA publications on bookkeeping, budget analysis, marketing, inventory, management, and much more. For all of this information, contact:

Consumer Information Center
Pueblo, CO 81009

The U.S. Department of Commerce's "Roadmap" Program provides assistance to small- and medium-sized companies by connecting them to programs and services within all federal agencies. Information is available on federal procurement, exporting, funding sources, franchising, product standards, industry data, and many other subjects. Contact:

Roadmap
Office of Business Liaison
Room 5898-C
U.S. Department of Commerce
Washington, DC 20230

If your business will be doing anything with food, following are some helpful publications. Also, be sure to check with your own state department of agriculture.

Requirements of Laws and Regulations Enforced by the U.S. Food and Drug Administration. This booklet is available from the Superintendent of Documents (address listed previously). Ask for HHA publication number (FDA) 85-1115.

The Safe Food Book: Your Kitchen Guide. A single copy is free from the Consumer Information Center (address listed previously). Ask for publication H&G242. Another booklet, *Recipes for Quantity Food Service,* is available from the Superintendent of Documents (address listed previously).

Small Business Development Centers (SBDCs) are excellent sources of help and information to a person just starting out. They can offer business plans, marketing aids, bookkeeping consultations, computer assistance, managerial and technical training, and assessment testing, among other services. SBDCs are usually located at major state universities and sometimes at private colleges.

Tennessee Valley Authority

If you live in Tennessee or the Appalachian regions of Alabama, Georgia, Kentucky, Mississippi, North Carolina, or Virginia, the TVA offers assistance that includes workshops, literature, promotion,

. . . .

brochure development and publication, media kits, typesetting, and photography. Contact:

TVA
Old City Hall 2C-41-B
601 West Summit Hill Drive
Knoxville, TN 37902

National Association for the Cottage Industry

The National Association for the Cottage Industry is an organization for people who work out of their homes, and its goal is to address the needs and concerns of the home-based work force. For membership information, send a SASE to this address:

National Association for the Cottage Industry
P.O. Box 14460
Chicago, IL 60614
Phone: 1-773-472-8116

APPENDIX E

. . . .

VOLUNTEERING

As we mentioned earlier, volunteering can be a very rewarding and enriching experience. You'll find that this isn't just busy work; rather, volunteering enables you to make wonderful use of your time and talents and may reward you with social and spiritual benefits. The places and ways in which you can volunteer are far too numerous for us to list, but following are a few places to begin. Check your phone book for local chapters of national organizations. You can volunteer in person, join any of these organizations, or send donations. All will be appreciated. At the end of this section, we list books you can refer to for further information regarding volunteering.

Some Places to Volunteer

American Cancer Society
American Legion
AMERICORPS
AMVETS
Big Brothers/Big Sisters of America
Boy Scouts/Girl Scouts of America
Boys and Girls Clubs
Campfire Boys and Girls
Chamber of Commerce
Charity of your choice
Elks Club

To keep a lamp burning, we have to keep putting oil in it.

—Mother Teresa

Fire departments
Food banks
Goodwill
Governor's office
Greenpeace
Hospitals
Junior League
Keep America Beautiful
Key Club
Kiwanis Club
Knights of Columbus
League of Latin American Citizens
Libraries
Lions Club
Lutheran Brotherhood
Make a Wish Foundation
Mayor's Office
National 4-H Council
Place of worship
Police stations
Prisons
Red Cross
Rotary Club
Royal Neighbors of America
Salvation Army
Schools
Slovene National Benefit Society
State and National Park Services
Telephone Pioneers
U.S. Army and Air Force
U.S. Navy

N*ever look down on anybody unless you are helping them up.*

—Reverend Jesse Jackson

United Business Owners of America
United Way
Veterans of Foreign Wars
Youth Volunteer Corp.

Some Activities to Volunteer

Adopt a grandmother or grandfather at a home for the elderly.

Adopt a school with your friends and tutor the students.

Ask an agency what it needs and do all you can to provide it.

Build shelves or provide/prepare food at a food bank.

Clean a beach, park, river, or highway.

Clean out your attic and donate clothing and goods to a shelter.

Deliver food to AIDS, elderly, or homebound patients.

Fulfill a wish for a needy family.

Give free blood pressure tests or vision or hearing tests.

Hold an educational seminar for teenage moms.

Mentor an at-risk teen.

Paint over graffiti.

Plant flowers in public places.

Practice job interviews with teens and challenged adults.

Read to a needy child or to an elderly or a homebound person.

Recycle fee-deposit items and give the cash to a worthy cause.

Serve lunch at a soup kitchen.

Tape-record books for learning disabled children or blind people.

Teach a child or group of children about something you love.

Teach someone to read.

Visit a veteran's home and share stories or play games.

What else can you do to help?

Volunteering Opportunities That May Take You Around the World

CEDAM International
(for underwater enthusiasts)

> One Fox Road
> Croton-on-Hudson, NY 10520
>> Phone: 1-914-271-5365
>> Fax: 1-914-271-4723
>> E-mail: cedamint@aol.com
>> Website: http://www.cedam.org

Founded in 1967, CEDAM International is involved in Conservation, Education, Diving, Archaeology, and Museum work. They welcome novice and experienced divers, explorers, underwater videographers and photographers as well as amateur and skilled naturalists and marine biologists. CEDAM volunteers bring back live fish for public aquariums.

Earthwatch
(no special skills required)

> 680 Mount Auburn Street
> P.O. Box 9104
> Watertown, MA 02272-9104
>> Phone: 1-617-926-8200 or 1-800-776-0188
>> Fax: 1-617-926-8532
>> E-mail: info@earthwatch.org

Founded in 1972, Earthwatch is the world's largest organization matching members of the public with scientific and conservation projects worldwide. You can be at any fitness level, choose to stay in hotels or to sleep on the ground, and possibly share cooking. Most teams have six to ten people. Outings last ten days to two weeks. Earthwatch wants people who are brimming with curiosity and commitment and who are willing to roll up their sleeves.

> **I**t *is our task in our time and in our generation to hand down undiminished to those who come after us, as was handed down to us by those who went before, the natural wealth and beauty which is ours.*
>
> **—John F. Kennedy**

Global Volunteers

(no special skills required)

> 375 East Little Canada Road
> St. Paul, MN 55117-1628
> Phone: 1-800-487-1074

Global Volunteers enables people like you to assist others around the world and, in the process, to significantly enhance your own life. You may teach conversational English to elementary, secondary, college, or adult students in classrooms or in small groups. You may build, repair, or paint facilities. Men and women of all ages and backgrounds can help with these projects.

Health Volunteers Overseas

(physicians, dentists, physical therapists, nurses, other health professionals)

> c/o Washington Station
> P.O. Box 65157
> Washington, DC 20035-5157

Phone: 1-202-296-0928
Fax: 1-202-296-8018
E-mail: hvo@aol.com

Health Volunteers Overseas is a private nonprofit organization committed to improving health care in developing countries. Volunteers teach as well as provide a professional health service.

Medical Ministry International

(health professionals and fix-it people)

MMI-USA
P.O. Box 940207
Plano, TX 75094
Phone: 1-972-437-1995
Fax: 1-972-237-1114
E-mail: mmitx@computek.net
Website: http://www.mmiusa.org/

MGM-Canada, Inc.
15 John Street North, Suite 301
Hamilton, Ontario L8R-1H1
Phone: 905.524-3544
Fax: 905.524-5400
E-mail: vwhz69a@prodigy.com

Medical Ministry International (in Canada the ministry is called Medical Group Missions) has a thirty-year history of providing opportunities for volunteers to work in one- or two-week medical, dental, surgical, or eye clinics, helping people who have little or no access to medical care. They see over 250,000 patients in over eighteen countries annually. This group is interdenominational, serving the poor in the name of Jesus. For more project information about needs for medicines, eyeglasses, computers, vehicles, and additional wish-list items, contact the above addresses.

APPENDIX F

. . . .

TRAVEL TIPS

Travel Agencies

AJS Travel (Fifty Plus Club)
(special group tours to certain places; individual tours anywhere in the world)
> 177 Beach 116th St.
> Rockaway Park, NY 11694
>> Phone: 1-800-221-5002 or 1-718-945-5900

Grand Travel
(tours for grandparents and school-age grandchildren; also includes aunts and uncles)
> 6900 Wisconsin Avenue, #706
> Chevy Chase, MD 20815
>> Phone: 1-800-247-7651 or 1-301-986-0790
>> Website: http://www.grandtrvl.com

Grand Circle Travel
(general)
> 347 Congress Street
> Boston, MA 02210
>> Phone: 1-800-221-2610 or 1-617-350-7500

Mayflower Tours
(general)
> 1225 Warren Avenue
> Downers Grove, IL 60515
>> Phone: 1-800-323-7604 or 1-630-960-3430

Saga Holidays, Ltd.

(general)

120 Boylston Street
Boston, MA 02116
Phone: 1-800-343-0273

Airlines

The airlines sell coupon books to people over age sixty-two (some younger). Certain restrictions apply regarding advance purchase, days of travel, etc. Special rates often apply to travel companions. Check with the individual airlines about their senior citizen travel clubs. Also, ask if you are getting the cheapest fare available. Check the Yellow Pages for the local numbers of national and foreign carriers.

National Airlines

America West	1-800-235-9292
	http://www.americawest.com
American	1-800-433-7300
	http://www.americanair.com
Continental	1-800-523-3273
	http://www.flycontinental.com
Delta	1-800-241-4141
	http://www.delta-air.com
Northwest	1-800-225-2525
	http://www.nwa.com
TWA	1-800-221-2000
	http://www.twa.com
United	1-800-241-6522
	http://www.ual.com

 HOW TO ENJOY YOUR RETIREMENT

| Western Pacific | 1-800-930-3030 |
| | http://www.westpac.com |

Foreign Airlines

Air Canada	1-800-776-3000
	http://www.aircanada.ca
British Airways	1-800-247-9297
	http://www.british-airways.com
Canadian	1-800-426-7000
	http://www.cdnair.ca
China	1-800-227-5118
	http://www.chinaairlines.com
KLM Royal Dutch	1-800-374-7747
	http://www.klm.nl
Mexicana	1-800-531-7921
	http://www.mexicana.com
SAS (Scandinavian)	1-800-221-2350
	http://www.flysas.com

Car Rental

Discounts are available to members of various senior citizen groups, e.g., AARP, airline and travel clubs, and hotel travel clubs. Ask about discounts when you make your reservation.

Alamo	1-800-327-9633
	http://www.goalamo.com
Avis	1-800-831-2847
	http://www.avis.com
Budget	1-800-527-0700
	http://www.budgetrentacar.com

. . . .

Dollar	1-800-800-4000
	http://www.dollarcar.com
Hertz	1-800-654-3131
	http://www.hertz.com
National	1-800-227-7368
	http://www.nationalcar.com
Thrifty	1-800-367-2277
	http://www.thrifty.com
Value	1-800-468-2583
	http://www.govalue.com

Cruises

Carnival	1-800-227-6482
	http://www.carnival.com
Cruise One	1-800-555-4732
	http://www.cruiseone.com
Cunard	1-800-528-6273
	http://www.cunardline.com
Holland America	1-800-426-0327
	http://www.hollandamerica.com
Norwegian	1-800-327-7030
	http://www.ncl.com
Premier	1-800-327-7113
	http://www.bigredboat.com
Royal Caribbean	1-800-327-6700
	http://www.royalcaribbean.com

Hotels

Check your Yellow Pages for the following hotels' local phone numbers or different 800 numbers if the 800 numbers given below do not work in your area. (Some 800-number companies only want to pay the charges for a certain state or a certain area. Others will accept charges from the whole United States.) Following are some questions to ask:

1. What organizations are entitled to discounts? (AARP, airline clubs, travel clubs, etc.)

2. Are there restrictions regarding age of traveler and age of companion?

3. What is the percent of discount?

4. What is the cost to join the hotel's own travel club or program?

5. Do traveling companions or grandchildren under age eighteen stay free?

6. Is there a free breakfast or discounted food? free newspaper, long distance calls, coffee or tea? a happy hour?

7. Must you reserve for yourself or through a travel agent?

8. What are the regions or states where this hotel chain operates?

9. Are there blackout periods or restrictions on days of the week, length of stay, or holiday stays?

Offers can change from time to time, so be sure to check what is current. Call or write ahead for a directory and information. (The initials TDD stand for **T**elecommunication **D**evice for the **D**eaf.)

Best Western International   1-800-528-1234
                             1-800-528-2222 (TDD)
                             http://www.bestwestern.com/best.html

Choice Hotels International 1-800-221-2222
1-800-228-3323 (TDD)

Comfort Inns and Suites   1-800-228-5150
http://www.comfortinn.com

Days Inns   1-800-329-7466
1-800-222-3297 (TDD)
http://www.daysinn.com
September Days Club

Doubletree Club Hotels   1-800-222-8733
http://www.doubletreehotels.com

Drury Inns   1-800-325-8300
http://www.drury-inn.com

EconoLodge   1-800-553-2666
http://www.hotelchoice.com

Economy Inns of America   1-800-826-0778

Embassy Suites/Granada Royale
1-800-362-2779
http://www.embassy-suites.com

Hampton Inns   1-800-426-7866
http://www.hampton-inn.com
Lifestyle 50 Club

Hilton Hotels   1-800-445-8667
http://www.hilton.com
Senior Honors Club

Holiday Inns   1-800-465-4329
http://www.holiday-inn.com
Alumni Program (1-800-258-6642)

Howard Johnson's Motor Lodges

        1-800-634-3464

        http://www.hojo.com

        Howard Johnson's Road Rally

Hyatt Hotels and Resorts   1-800-233-1234

        http://www.hyatt.com

Inns Suites (in Arizona and California)

        1-800-842-4242

        http://www.istempe@allmail.com

Knights Inns/Arborgate Inn/Knights Courts/Knights Stops
(mostly in the south and east; call for free directory)

        1-800-722-7220

        http://www.knightsinns.com

La Quinta Motor Inns   1-800-531-5900

        http://www.laquinta.com

Marriott Hotels and Resort Suites

        1-800-228-9290

        http://www.marriott.com

Quality Inns   1-800-228-5151

        http://www.hotelchoice.com

Radisson Hotels International

        1-800-333-3333

        http://www.radisson.com

Ramada International Hotels & Resorts

        1-800-228-2828

        1-800-228-3232 (TDD)

        http://www.ramada.com/ramada.html

Red Roof Inns   1-800-843-7663

        http://www.redroof.com

Renaissance Hotels & Resort

1-800-468-3571

1-800-833-4747 (TDD)

http://www.renaissancehotels.com

Rodeway Inns   1-800-424-6423

http://www.hotelchoice.com

Sheraton Hotels   1-800-325-3535 (U.S. and Canada)

http://www.sheraton.com

Shoney's Inns   1-800-222-2222 (in the Southwest)

http://www.shoneysinns.com

Sonesta International Hotels

1-800-766-3782

http://www.sonesta.com

Travelodge   1-800-255-3050

http://www.travelodge.com

Westin Hotels & Resorts   1-800-228-3000

http://www.westin.com

Vacation Rental Homes

At Home Abroad   1-212-421-9165

Interhome   1-201-882-6864

Rent a Home International   1-800-488-7368

http://www.rentavilla.com

Vacation Rental Managers Association

1-800-871-8762

http://www.vrma.com

Villas International   1-800-221-2260

Contact Information for State and Local Visitors Bureaus

Alabama

Alabama Bureau of Tourism and Travel

401 Adams Avenue

P.O. Box 4927

Montgomery, AL 36103

Phone: 1-334-242-4169

or 1-800-ALA-BAMA (252-2262)

E-mail: alabama@mont.mindspring.com

Website: http://www.touralabama.com

Alaska

Alaska Division of Tourism

P.O. Box 110801

Juno, AK 99811

Phone: 1-907-465-2010 or 1-907-456-2012

E-mail: gonorth@commerce.state.ak.us

Website: http://www.state.ak.us

Arizona

Arizona Office of Tourism

1100 West Washington Street

Phoenix, AZ 85007

Phone: 1-602-542-8687

or 1-800-842-8257

Arkansas

Department of Parks and Tourism

One Capitol Mall

Little Rock, AR 72201

Phone: 1-501-371-7777

or 1-800-NATURAL (628-8725)

Website: http://www.ono.com/arkansas

California

California State Board of Tourism

801 K Street, #1600

Sacramento, CA 95814

Phone: 1-916-322-2881

or 1-800-862-2543

Website: http://www.gocalif.ca.gov

Colorado

(At this time, there is no statewide visitors bureau.)

Avon Chamber of Commerce

P.O. Box 1437

Avon, CO 81620

Phone: 1-970-949-5189

Website: http://www.vail.net/chamber//

Denver Metro Convention and Visitors Bureau

1555 California Street, #300

Denver, CO 80202

Phone: 1-303-892-1112

or 1-800-645-3446

Website: http://www.denver.org

Greeley Convention and Visitors Bureau

1407 Eighth Avenue

Greeley, CO 80631

Phone: 1-970-352-3566

or 1-800-449-3866

Website: http://www.greeleychamber.com

Montrose Visitor and Convention Bureau
P.O. Box 335
Montrose, CO 81402
Phone: 1-970-249-5000
or 1-800-873-0244

Pueblo Convention and Visitors Council
302 North Santa Fe Avenue
Pueblo, CO 81003
Phone: 1-719-542-1704
or 1-719-542-1705
Website: http://www.pueblo.org

Connecticut

Connecticut State Board of Tourism
Department of Economic Development, Tourism Division
505 Hudson Street
Hartford, CT 06106
Phone: 1-800-CT-BOUND (282-6863)
Website: http://www.state.ct.us/tourism.htm

Delaware

Delaware Tourism Office
99 Kings Highway
P.O. Box 1401
Dover, DE 19901
Phone: 1-302-739-4271
or 1-800-441-8846
Website: http://www.state.de.us

District of Columbia

Washington DC Convention and Visitors Association
1212 New York Avenue, NW, #600
Washington, DC 20005

Phone: 1-202-789-7000

Website: http://www.washington.org

Florida

Florida State Board of Tourism

Collins Building

107 West Gaines Street

Tallahassee, FL 32399

Phone: 1-888-735-2872

Website: http://www.flausa.com

Georgia

Georgia State Board of Tourism

P.O. Box 1776

Atlanta, GA 30301

Phone: 1-404-656-3590

or 1-800-847-4842

Website: http://www.gomm.com

Hawaii

Hawaii State Board of Tourism

2270 Kalakaua Avenue, #801

Honolulu, HI 96815

Phone: 1-808-923-1811

or 1-800-464-2924

Website: http://www.gohawaii.com

Idaho

Idaho Division of Travel Promotion

700 West State Street

Boise, ID 83720

Phone: 1-208-334-2470

or 1-800-635-7820

Website: http://www.idoc.state.id.us

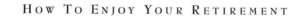

Illinois

Illinois State Board of Tourism

100 West Randolph Street, Room 3-400

Chicago, IL 60601

Phone: 1-312-280-5740

or 1-800-223-0121

Website: http://www.enjoyillinois.com

Indiana

Indiana State Board of Tourism

One North Capitol, #700

Indianapolis, IN 46204

Phone: 1-317-232-8860

or 1-800-289-6646

Website: http://www.indianatourism.com

Iowa

Iowa State Department of Tourism

200 East Grand Avenue

Des Moines, IA 50309

Phone: 1-515-281-3100

or 1-800-345-IOWA (345-4692)

and 1-888-472-6035

Website: http://www.state.ia.us.

Kansas

Kansas State Board of Tourism

700 Southwest Harrison Street, #1300

Topeka, KS 66603

Phone: 1-913-296-2009

or 1-800-2KANSAS (252-6727)

Website: http://www.kansascommerce.com

Kentucky

Kentucky Department of Travel
Capital Plaza Tower, Floor 22
500 Metro Street
Frankfort, KY 40601

> Phone: 1-502-564-4930
>> or 1-800-225-TRIP (225-8747)
> E-mail: travel@tourpost@msmail.state.ky.us
> Website: http://www.state.ky.us/tour/tour.html

Louisiana

Louisiana State Board of Tourism
P.O. Box 94291
Baton Rouge, LA 70804

> Phone: 1-504-342-8119
>> or 1-800-33GUMBO (334-8626)
> Website: http://www.louisianatourism.com

Maine

The Maine Publicity Bureau
P.O. Box 2300
Hallowell, ME 04347

> Phone: 1-207-623-0363
> Website: http://www.visitmaine.com

Maryland

Maryland State Board of Tourism
217 East Redwood Street
Baltimore, MD 21201

> Phone: 1-410-333-6611
>> or 1-800-543-1036
> Website: http://www.mdisfun.org

Massachusetts

Massachusetts Office of Travel and Tourism
100 Cambridge Street, Floor 13
Boston, MA 02202
Phone: 1-617-727-3201
or 1-800-447-6277
Website: http://www.mass.travel.com

Michigan

Michigan State Board of Tourism
P.O. Box 30226
Lansing, MI 48909
Phone: 1-800-543-2937
E-mail: atwoodt@state.mi.us
Website: http://www.michigan.org

Minnesota

Minnesota Office of Tourism
100 Metro Square
St. Paul, MN 55101
Phone: 1-612-296-5029
or 1-800-657-3700
Website: http://www.exploreminnesota.com

Mississippi

Mississippi Department of Tourism Development
P.O. Box 849
Jackson, MS 39205
Phone: 1-601-359-3297
or 1-800-927-6378
Website: http://www.mississippi.org

Missouri

Missouri State Board of Tourism
P.O. Box 1055
Truman State Office Bldg.
Jefferson City, MO 65102
Phone: 1-314-751-4133
or 1-800-877-1234
Website: http://www.ecoder.state.mo.us/tourism/

Montana

Travel Montana
1424 Ninth Avenue
Helena, MT 59620
Phone: 1-406-444-2654
or 1-800-548-3390
Website: http://www.travel.mt.gov/

Nebraska

Nebraska Tourism
P.O. Box 94666
Lincoln, NE 68509
Phone: 1-402-471-3798
or 1-800-228-4307
Website: http://www.ded.state.ne.us/tourism.html

Nevada

Nevada State Board of Tourism
Capitol Complex
Carson City, NV 89710
Phone: 1-800-NEVADA-8 (638-2328)

New Hampshire

New Hampshire Tourism
172 Pembroke Road
P.O. Box 1856
Concord, NH 03302
Phone: 1-603-271-2343 (Travel Counselors)
1-800-386-4664 (Kits)
Website: http://www.visitnh.gov

New Jersey

State of New Jersey Division of Travel and Tourism
20 West State Street CN826
Trenton, NJ 08625
Phone: 1-609-292-2470
or 1-800-JERSEY7 (537-7397)
Website: http://www.state.nj.us

New Mexico

New Mexico State Board of Tourism
491 Old Santa Fe Trail
Santa Fe, NM 87503
Phone: 1-505-827-0291
or 1-800-545-2040
Website: http://www.newmexico.org/

New York

Empire State Development, Division of Tourism
One Commerce Plaza
Albany, NY 12245
Phone: 1-518-474-4116
or 1-800-225-5697
E-mail: iloveny@empire.state.ny.us
Website: http://iloveny.state.ny.us

North Carolina

North Carolina State Board of Tourism

301 North Wilmington Street

Raleigh, NC 27601

> Phone: 1-919-733-4171
>> or 1-800-VISIT-NC (847-4862)
> Website: http://www.visitnc.com

North Dakota

North Dakota Tourism Department

604 East Boulevard

Bismarck, ND 58505

> Phone: 1-701-328-2525
>> or 1-800-435-5663
> E-mail: msmail.phertz@ranch.state.nd.us
> Website: http://www.ndtourism.com

Ohio

Ohio Division of Travel and Tourism

77 S. High Street

P.O. Box 1001

Columbus, OH 43216

> Phone: 1-614-466-8844
>> or 1-800-BUCKEYE (282-5393)
> Website: http://www.ohiotourism.com

Oklahoma

Oklahoma Tourism and Recreation Department

P.O. Box 52002

Oklahoma City, OK 73152

> Phone: 1-405-521-2406
>> or 1-405-522-3935
> Website: http://www.otrd.state.ok.us/

Oregon

> Oregon Tourism Division
> 775 Summer Street, NE
> Salem, OR 97310
> > Phone: 1-503-373-1200
> > > or 1-800-547-7842
> > Website: http://www.traveloregon.com

Pennsylvania

> Pennsylvania Office of Travel Marketing
> 456 Forum Building
> Harrisburg, PA 17120
> > Phone: 1-717-787-5453
> > > or 1-800-VISITPA (847-4872)
> > Website: http://www.state.pa.us

Rhode Island

> Rhode Island State Board of Tourism
> 1 West Exchange Street
> Providence, RI 02903
> > Phone: 1-401-277-2601
> > > or 1-800-556-2484
> > Website: http://www.visitrhodeisland.com

South Carolina

> South Carolina Department of Parks, Recreation, and Tourism
> 1205 Pendleton Street, #106
> P.O. Box 71
> Columbia, SC 29202
> > Phone: 1-803-734-0122
> > > or 1-800-872-3505

South Dakota

South Dakota State Board of Tourism
711 East Wells Avenue
Capitol Lake Plaza
Pierre, SD 57501
> Phone: 1-605-773-3301
> > or 1-800-872-6190
> Website: http://www.state.sd.us

Tennessee

Tennessee Department of Tourist Development
320 Sixth Avenue North
Nashville, TN 37202
> Phone: 1-615-741-2158
> > or 1-800-836-6200
> Website: http://www.state.tn.us

Texas

Texas Department of Commerce—Tourism Division
Box 12728
Capitol Station
Austin, TX 78711
> Phone: 1-512-462-9191
> Website: http://www.traveltex.com

Utah

Utah State Board of Tourism
Council Hall, Capitol Hill
Salt Lake City, UT 84114
> Phone: 1-801-538-1030
> Website: http://www.utah.com

Vermont

Vermont Department of Travel and Tourism
134 State Street
Montpelier, VT 05602
Phone: 1-802-828-3236
or 1-800-837-6668
Website: http://www.travel-vermont.com

Virginia

Virginia Division of Tourism
901 East Byrd Street
Richmond, VA 23919
Phone: 1-804-786-4484
Website: http://www.virginia.org

Washington

Washington State Board of Tourism
General Administration Building, Suite 101
Olympia, WA 98504
Phone: 1-206-753-5600
or 1-800-544-1800
Website: http://www.tourism.wa.gov

West Virginia

West Virginia State Board of Tourism
2101 Washington Street East
Charleston, WV 25305
Phone: 1-304-558-2286
or 1-800-225-5982
Website: http://www.state.wv.us/tourism/default.htm

Wisconsin

Wisconsin Tourism Development
P.O. Box 7970
Madison, WI 53702
>Phone: 1-608-266-7621
>>or 1-800-432-TRIP (432-8747)
>Website: http://www.tourism.state.wi.us/

Wyoming

Wyoming State Board of Tourism
I-25 (Interstate 25) at College Drive
Cheyenne, WY 82002
>Phone: 1-307-777-7777
>>or 1-800-CALL-WYO (225-5996)
>Website:
>>http://www.state.wy.us/commerce/tourism/index.htm

Hiking Information Sources

Continental Divide Trail

Rio Grande National Forest
1803 West Highway 160
Monte Vista, CO 81144
>Phone: 1-719-852-5941

San Juan National Forest
701 Camino del Rio, Room 301
Durango, CO 81301
>Phone: 1-970-247-4874

Greenbrier River Trail

Star Route

Box 125

Caldwell, WV 24925

Phone: 1-304-645-2760

Idaho Centennial Trail

Idaho Department of Parks and Recreation

Statehouse Mail

Boise, ID 83720

Phone: 1-208-384-4240

Marble Mountain Wilderness

U.S. Forest Service

Forest Supervisor's Office

1312 Fairlane Road

Yreka, CA 96097

Phone: 1-916-842-6131

Mariscal Canyon Trail

Big Bend National Park

Texas 79834

Phone: 1-915-477-2251

Ozark Trail

Ozark National Scenic Riverway

P.O. Box 490

Van Buren, MO 63965

Phone: 1-573-323-4236

Smartsbrook Trail

Pemigewasset District Ranger

White Mountain National Forest

Route 3, Box 15

Plymouth, NH 03264

Phone: 1-603-536-1310

Superior Hiking Trail

Superior Hiking Trail Association

P.O. Box 4

Two Harbors, MN 55616

Phone: 1-218-834-2700

Additional Reading and Internet Sites Related to Travel

BOOKS

Field Guide to Mysterious Places of Eastern North America by Salvatore M. Trento (Owl Books, $18.95). This book gives information about enigmatic sites: caves, tunnels, and other places linked to unexplained phenomena. Maps, line drawings, and photos illustrate the enduring intrigue of these destinations.

Mountain Search and Rescue Techniques by Bill May. Although this book has gone out of print, check for it in your local library. Written in 1972, it is still highly regarded as a great text for search and rescue application The book offers thorough discussion of topics ranging from knots to missing person search patterns to technical rock rescues.

Off the Beaten Path: A Guide to More Than 1,000 Scenic and Interesting Places Still Uncrowded and Inviting by Readers Digest is available by calling 1-800-234-9000. The cost is $23.97 plus $4.49 for shipping (plus tax where applicable). This book lists, state by state, all kinds of little-known places to visit.

Smithsonian's Great Battles and Battlefields of the Civil War: A Field Guide by Jay Wertz and Edwin C. Bears (William Morrow, $42.00). This book, based on an award-winning video series by

 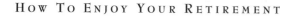

Mastervision, combines history with directions and travel information about Civil War sites.

Trouble-Free Travel: And What To Do When Things Go Wrong by Stephen Colwell and Ann Shulman (Nolo Press, $14.95). This book provides tips for handling problems and avoiding hassles while traveling.

Trailer Life magazine, 2575 Vista Del Mar, Ventura, CA 93001 (1-805-667-4100). For subscription information, write to P.O. Box 55793, Boulder, CO 80328-5793.

Also, Woodall Publishing offers dozens of guides that provide RV (recreational vehicle or motorhome), tenting, and campground information for different regions and interests. Contact Woodall Publishing Corporation, 13975 West Polo Trail Drive, Lake Forest, IL 60045-5000, or visit their website at http://www.woodals.com .

CATALOGS

Bolder Adventures catalog lists trips to Southeast Asia (1-800-642-2742).

Butterfield & Robinson catalog lists biking and walking tours (1-800-678-1147).

Club America has a Vacations Planner that describes holidays to the Caribbean and Mexico. The planner is available from your travel agent.

ElderTreks catalog specializes in trips for older travelers (1-800-741-7956).

Interhostel catalog lists international study programs for travelers age fifty and older (1-800-733-9753 or 1-603-862-1147).

INTERNET

Interhostel offers international study programs for travelers age fifty and older; website: http://www.learn.unh.edu .

Journeywoman is a website full of tips and information designed to encourage women to travel; website: http://www.journeywoman.com .

National Parks and Conservation Association website: http://www.npca.org/home/npca/ .

ParkNet is a comprehensive site where you can search by park name, state, or region to find maps, entrance fees, and information on how to preserve and support the park system; website: http://www.nps.gov .

A P P E N D I X   G

. . . .

A D D I T I O N A L
I N F O R M A T I O N
R E S O U R C E S

AGING

Aging Network Services

4400 East-West Highway #907

Bethesda, MD 20814

Phone: 1-301-657-4329

Aging Network Services offers counseling on care management for aging relatives and concerned family members. Call or write for brochures and information on fees.

National Council on Aging

409 Third Street, SW

Washington, DC 0024

Phone: 1-202-479-1200 (for catalog of publications)

ALLERGIES

Allergy Resources

P.O. Box 156

Guffey, CO 80202

Phone: 1-800-USE-FLAX (873-3529)

The Gluten-Free Pantry

P.O. Box 881

Glastonbury, CT 06033-0881

Phone: 1-860-633-3826

This mail order company sells 15 gluten-free baking mixes for brownies, pasta, muffins, bagels, breads, and more.

ARTHRITIS

Arthritis Foundation
P.O. Box 19000
Atlanta, GA 30326
Phone: 1-800-283-7800
Website: http://www.arthritis.org

The Arthritis Foundation offers self-help courses, exercise programs, support groups, and pamphlets on arthritis and its management. Check your White Pages for a local chapter or contact the national office.

CANCER

American Cancer Society
Phone: 1-800-227-2345

American Prostate Society
1340F Charwood Road
Hanover, MD 21076
Phone: 1-410-859-3735

"Man to Man" is an APS support group for men with prostate cancer.

Cancer Information Services
Office of Cancer Communications
Building 31, Room 10A18
Bethesda, MD 20892
Phone: 1-800-4-CANCER (422-6237)

Cancer Information Services offers answers to questions regarding causes, symptoms, and treatment of cancer; gives referrals to cancer specialists and treatment studies; and offers free publications.

Inquiries about Diethylstilbestrol (DES)
1-800-337-9288
Website: http://www.ITVS.org/babyg

Organization called Y-ME
(Breast Cancer Support Program)
        18220 Harwood Avenue
        Homewood, IL 60430
                Phone: 1-800-221-2141 (9 A.M.–5 P.M. CST Weekdays)
                Emergency 24-Hour Hotline: 1-708-799-8228

CARPAL TUNNEL

Center for Carpal Tunnel Studies
        10555 North Tatum Boulevard, Suite A-104
        Paradise Valley, AZ 85253
Dr. Benjamin Sucher has a one-week program designed to resolve carpal tunnel conditions.

CHILDREN
Partnership for a Drug-Free America
        Phone: 1-800-624-0100
Parents can get a free handbook about drugs.

Save The Children Headquarters
        54 Wilton Road
        Westport, CT 06880
                Phone: 1-800-243-5075

Shriners Hospital for Crippled Children
        Phone: 1-800-237-5055

DIABETES
American Diabetes Association
        Phone: 1-800-232-3472
                or 1-703-549-1500
The American Diabetes Association offers a wealth of educational literature plus counseling, lectures, and workshops. Check your White Pages for a local listing.

EARS AND EYES

American Speech-Language-Hearing Association

> 10801 Rockville Pike
> Rockville, MD 20852
> > Phone: 1-800-638-8255
> > or 1-301-897-8682

This association offers information on hearing aids, hearing loss, and communication problems. It also provides lists of certified audiologists and speech pathologists in each state.

National Information Center on Deafness

> Gallaudet University
> 800 Florida Avenue, NE
> Washington, DC 20002
> > Phone: 1-202-651-5051 (voice)
> > or 1-202-651-5052 (TDD)

The NICD offers information on assistive devices for deaf and hard-of-hearing people. It also offers a set of six publications designed for elderly people and available for a nominal fee.

Self Help for Hard of Hearing People, Inc. (SHHH)

> 7800 Wisconsin Avenue
> Bethesda, MD 20814
> > Phone: 1-301-657-2248 (voice)
> > or 1-301-657-2249 (TDD)

SHHH offers a bi-monthly journal, holds annual conventions, and has local chapters and groups. Write or call for membership information.

American Printing House for the Blind

(braille and large-type books)
> 1839 Frankfort Avenue
> P.O. Box 6085

Louisville, KY 40206

      Phone: 1-800-223-1839

National Society to Prevent Blindness

500 East Remington Road

Schaumburg, IL 60173

      Phone: 1-800-331-2020

This national society offers a variety of materials on eye health and safety, including information on cataracts, glaucoma, and diabetic retinopathy. Also call the National Center for Sight at 1-800-221-3004.

ENVIRONMENT

Greenpeace

(environmental specialists)

1436 U Street, NW

Washington, DC 20009

Phone: 1-800-326-0959

National Arbor Day Foundation

(trees and tree planting)

100 Arbor Avenue

Nebraska City, NE 68410

National Audubon Society

(bird specialists)

700 Broadway

New York, NY 10003

      Phone: 1-212-979-3000

Sierra Club

(trees and wilderness)

730 Polk Street

San Francisco, CA 94109

      Phone: 1-800-935-1056

. . . .

HEAD AND NECK PAIN

American Academy of Otolaryngology
(head and neck surgery)

> 1 Prince Street
> Alexandria, VA 22314
> Phone: 1-703-836-4444

This academy offers free patient education leaflets on ear, nose, and throat problems. Send a self-addressed, stamped, business-size envelope and request the leaflet on your problem.

HEALTH REFERRAL

National Health Information Center
(health referral service)

> ODPHP
> P.O. Box 1133
> Washington, DC 20013
> Phone: 1-800-336-4797
> or 1-301-565-4167

ODPHP stands for Office of Disease Prevention and Health Promotion. This office will refer you to organizations that can respond to your specific health questions.

HEART HEALTH

American Heart Association

> 7320 Greenville Avenue
> Dallas, TX 75231
> Phone: 1-800-AHA-USA-1 (242-8721)

The American Heart Association offers books and information regarding heart attack prevention and rehabilitation. Check your White Pages for a local listing.

MEDICINE
Flu and Pneumonia Shot Information
Contact your doctor or health clinic, or call the National Institute on Aging at 1-800-222-2225 or the American Lung Association at 1-800-LUNG-USA (586-4872).

National Council on Patient Information and Education
> Before You Take It
> 666 Eleventh Street, NW, Suite 810
> Washington, DC 20001

This national council offers two free brochures—*Medicine: Before You Take It, Talk About It* and *Prescription Medicine and You: A Consumer's Guide.* Send a #10, self-addressed, stamped envelope for each brochure. (Send two envelopes if you want both brochures.)

MENTAL HEALTH
Alzheimers Association
> 919 North Michigan Avenue, Suite 1000
> Chicago, IL 60611
> > Phone: 1-800-272-3900 or 1-312-335-8700
> > Website: http://www.alz.org

National Mental Health Association
> 1021 Prince Street
> Alexandria, VA 22314
> > Phone: 1-800-969-6642

MULTIPLE SCLEROSIS
National Multiple Sclerosis Society
> 733 Third Avenue
> New York, NY 10017
> > Phone: 1-800 LEARN-MS (532-7667)

OSTEOPOROSIS

American College of Obstetricians and Gynecologists
Resource Center, #48
409 Twelfth Street, SW
Washington, DC 20024

PARKINSON'S DISEASE

The following organizations offer pamphlets for patients with
Parkinson's Disease and their families.

American Parkinson's Disease Association
60 Bay Street
Staten Island, NY 10301
Phone: 1-800-223-2732

National Parkinson Foundation
1501 Northwest Ninth Avenue
Miami, FL 33136
Phone: 1-800-327-4545
or 1-305-547-6666

Parkinson's Disease Foundation
Columbia Presbyterian Medical Research Center
William Black Research Building
650 West 168th Street
New York, NY 10032
Phone: 1-212-525-5851

Parkinson Support Groups of America
11376 Cherry Hill Road, Apartment 204
Beltsville, MD 20705
Phone: 1-301-937-1545

SPORTS

National Senior Sports Association (NSSA)

167 Old Post Road

Southport, CT 06490

Phone: 1-800-282-6772

The NSSA offers recreational and competitive sports (including golf and tennis) events and trips; discounts on sports equipment, apparel, publications, and leisure products; and Gold Card membership. They have a monthly newsletter, a name-and-address list of members to visit when traveling, and information on where you can play your sport at international resorts overseas.

Over the Hill Gang International

3310 Cedar Heights Drive

Colorado Springs, CO 80904

Phone: 1-719-685-4656

This group offers sports, travel, and adventures at a discount for people age fifty and over (spouses of any age). Over three thousand members make up fifteen "gangs" in various cities. They enjoy ballooning, camping, canoeing, fishing, biking, scuba diving, ski trips, surfing, and more. Call or write for information.

Senior Games Association

14323 South Outer Forty Road, Suite N300

Chesterfield, MO 63017

Phone: 1-314-621-5545

The Senior Games Association offers biennial event for athletes age fifty-five and over. Contact local Senior Olympics or the national group.

U.S. Coast Guard

(boating safety)

Consumer Information Line

Phone: 1-800-368-5647

The U.S. Coast Guard phone source offers information about boating safety classes, radio licenses, and navigation rules.

Van Der Meer Tennis Center

>P.O. Box 5902
>Hilton Head Island, SC 29938
>>Phone: 1-800-845-6138
>>>or 1-803-785-8388

This tennis center offers a five-day Seniors Clinic for players age forty-five and over, with personalized evaluation and instruction by Dennis Van Der Meer.

STROKE

National Institute of Neurological Disorders and Stroke (NINDS)

>Office of Scientific and Health Reports
>Building 31, Room 8A06
>31 Center Drive
>Bethesda, MD 20892
>>Phone: 1-800-352-9424

This institute offers information on prevention of nervous system disorders and stroke. For information on treatment or rehabilitation services, you might also call a university teaching hospital in your area.

National Stroke Association

>8480 East Orchard Road, Suite 1000
>Englewood, CO 80111
>>Phone: 1-800-STROKES (787-6537)

APPENDIX H

. . . .

ADDITIONAL READING SUGGESTIONS

Age Wave: Choices & Challenges for Our New Future by Ken Dychtwald (Bantam Books, $13.95). Relates through a comprehensive analysis the consequences, now and in the next decades, of the aging Baby Boom.

Aging in Good Health: A Complete Essential Medical Guide for Men and Women over Fifty and Their Families by Mark Beers, M.D. and Stephen K. Urice (Pocket Books, $10.00). The title is self-explanatory.

Awakening at Midlife: Realizing Your Potential for Growth and Change by Kathleen A. Brehony (Riverhead Books, $24.95). Contains suggestions for strategies that will help you through the transition into a richer and more meaningful second half of your life.

Buying Your Vacation Home: For Fun and Profit by Ruth Rejnis and Claire Walter (Dearborn Financial Publishing, $19.95). This book describes how and where to find, buy, finance, use, rent, and ultimately sell that second home. It discusses the pros and cons of condos, single family homes, raw land, RVs, and even houseboats.

Everything to Gain: Making the Most of the Rest of Your Life by Jimmy Carter and Rosalynn Carter (Fawcett, $4.95). The Carters tell how they adjusted to life after the White House and how they started working with Habitat for Humanity and other organizations. Many volunteer organizations are described.

Forty Reasons Why Life Is More Fun after the Big 40: An Encourager by Liz Curtis Higgs (Thomas Nelson Publishers, $10.99). Women over forty share views on joys and challenges of life after forty.

Free Stuff for Seniors by Matthew Lesko, edited by Andrew Naprawa (Information U.S.A., Inc., $19.95). The title says it all.

Getting Over Getting Older: An Intimate Journey by Letty Cottin Pogrebin (Berkley Publishing Group, $13.00). A book written to help alleviate the fears and celebrate the possibilities of getting older.

Keys to Volunteering by Elizabeth Vierck and Betsy Vierck (Barrons Educational Series, $6.95). Volunteering can be a very rewarding experience and a good way to remain a vital member of the community. This book is part of Barron's *Keys to Retirement Planning.*

Life Begins at 50: A Handbook for Creative Retirement Planning by Leonard J. Hansen (Barrons Educational Series, $12.95). The title says it.

Look Like a Winner after 50 with Care, Color, and Style by Jo Peddicord (Gold Aspen Publishing, $15.95). This book provides practical solutions for makeup, clothing, skin care, and fashion needs, especially for Baby Boomers turned grandmothers.

Retire and Thrive: Remarkable People Share Their Creative, Productive, and Profitable Retirement Strategies by Robert K. Otterbourg (Kiplinger Books, $15.00). The title says it.

Retirement Living Communities: A National Directory by Deborah Freundlich (Macmillan, $24.95). Listed state by state are over four hundred communities that offer high-quality independent living and a full range of health care services.

Retirement on a Shoestring by John Howells (Gateway Books, $8.95). Provides strategies for saving money and stretching your Social Security check as well as reducing the danger of crime.

10 Minute Guide to Retirement for Women by Kerry Hannon (Macmillan, $10.95). A book of financial tips on how to allocate your investments in employer pension plans and IRAs, how to choose medical insurance and long-term care policies, how to take advantage of the equity in your home to gain additional income, and much more.

The Work-at-Home Sourcebook: How to Find "At-Home" Work That's Right for You by Lynie Arden (Live Oak Publications, $19.95). Lists over one thousand job opportunities in addition to home business opportunities and other options.

You're Only Old Once! by Dr. Seuss (Random House, $18.00). A book written in Dr. Seuss–style for older readers.

INDEX

FEEDBACK FORM/SIDE 1
PLEASE STAY IN TOUCH

CAN YOU UPDATE INFORMATION IN THIS BOOK?

Write name of company or person: _____

Found on what page in this book: _____

What changed?
Give only the new information.

Address: _____

_____

Phone number: _____

Fax number: _____

E-mail address: _____

Website address: _____

Other new information:

MAIL OR FAX THIS FORM TO US AT THE PUBLISHER'S

Mail: Tricia Wagner & Barbara Day
            c/o VanderWyk & Burnham
            PO Box 2789
            Acton, MA 01720

Fax: (978) 263-7553

OR SEND US AN E-MAIL

In the "Subject" line, type: Retirement News
Send your message to: publicom@tiac.net

8/98

P L E A S E S T A Y I N T O U C H

HOW DID YOU LEARN ABOUT THIS BOOK?
Circle one:

> article or review
>
> advertisement
>
> word of mouth
>
> received as gift
>
> saw in store
>
> found in library

What do you like best about this book?

What do you like least about this book?

Is there anything you would like added to this book when we do a new edition?

What age range are you in?
Circle one:

below 45	56–65	76–85
45–55	66–75	86 and up

(See side 1 for our address, fax, and e-mail information.)